NEW TESTAMENT

EVERYDAY BIBLE STUDY SERIES

NEW TESTAMENT

EVERYDAY BIBLE STUDY SERIES

ROMANS

SCOT MCKNIGHT

QUESTIONS WRITTEN BY

BECKY CASTLE MILLER

New Testament Everyday Bible Study Series: Romans

Requests for information should be addressed to:
HarperChristian Resources, 3900 Sparks Dr. SE, Grand Rapids, Michigan 49546

ISBN 978-0-310-12941-7 (softcover)
ISBN 978-0-310-12942-4 (ebook)

HarperChristian Resources titles may be purchased in bulk for church, business, fundraising, or ministry use. For information, please e-mail ResourceSpecialist@ChurchSource.com.

First Printing February 2023 / Printed in the United States of America

CONTENTS

For Northern MANT 2016

GENERAL INTRODUCTION

Christians make a claim for the Bible not made of any other book. Or, since the Bible is a library shelf of many authors, it's a claim we make of no other shelf of books. We claim that God worked in each of the authors as they were writing so that what was scratched on papyrus expressed what God wanted communicated to the people of God. Which makes the New Testament (NT) a book unlike any other book. Which is why Christians are reading the NT almost two thousand years later with great delight. These books have the power to instruct us and to rebuke us and to correct us and to train us to walk with God every day. We read these books because God speaks to us in them.

Developing a routine of reading the Bible with an open heart, a receptive mind, and a flexible will is the why of the *New Testament Everyday Bible Studies*. But not every day will be the same. Some days we pause and take it in and other days we stop and repent and lament and open ourselves to God's restoring graces. No one word suffices for what the Bible does to us. In fact, the Bible's view of the Bible can be found by reading Psalm 119, the longest chapter in the Bible with 176 verses! It is a meditation on eight terms for what the Bible is and what the Bible does to those who listen and read it. Its laws (*torah*) instruct us, its laws (*mishpat*) order us, its statutes direct us, its precepts inform us, its decrees guide us, its commands compel us, its words speak to us, and its promises comfort us, and it is no wonder that the author can sum all eight up as the "way" (119:3, 37). Each of those terms still speaks to what happens when we open our minds to the Word of God.

Every day with the Bible then is new because our timeless and timely God communes with us in our daily lives in our world and in our time. Just as God spoke to Jesus in Galilee and Paul in Ephesus and John on Patmos. These various contexts help us hear God in our context so the *New Testament Everyday Bible Studies* will often delve into contexts.

Most of us now have a Bible on our devices. We may well have several translations available to us everywhere we go every day. To hear those words we are summoned by God to open the Bible, to attune our hearts to God, and to listen to what God says. My prayer is that these daily study guides will help each of us become daily Bible readers attentive to the mind of God.

INTRODUCTION: READING PAUL'S LETTER TO THE ROMANS

It's easy to get lost in Romans, and it's even easier for professors and pastors. The number of books produced each year about Paul boggles the mind. No one can keep up, and each year seems to harden the divisions between viewpoints about Paul. In a recent book about preaching Paul, four viewpoints were presented; in another book, five views were presented, and they were not entirely the same as the four; and in another book one can read how various ethnic groups around the world read Paul! I know these facts because I was involved in each book (see list of sources below).

We begin with this observation: Romans has lots and lots of theory. Put in our terms, lots and lots of theology and doctrine. Paul is arguing for theological truth with those who don't agree with him, so in reading Romans be prepared for some obscure terms and some sharp corners.

Romans is the most important letter of Paul's, and it is the most influential document in the New Testament for the formation of what Christians believe today. Our statements of faith and our evangelism tracts are rooted in what Paul says about salvation in the Letter to the Romans.

There are four parts to the letter. Most divide Romans into chapters 1–4, 5–8, 9–11, and 12–16. Most also read the whole letter as a theological statement about salvation and justification. Some see those four sections of Romans as Sin, Salvation, History, and Practice. Most, too, ignore the importance of the pastoral statements of the final five chapters (12–16). They can be excused for being worn out after reading the intensity of the first eleven chapters. Tired or worn out we may be, no matter—Paul was not, and neither were the house churches in Rome when they heard this letter read aloud (probably by Phoebe).

It is clear that Romans is about redemption, but in this study guide you will see that Romans is about peace, too. Peace between embattled Christians battling one another over who's in charge. One quick read of Romans 14–16 reveals the pastoral context of this letter, and no reading of Romans 1–11 that ignores 14–16 will catch the Pauline drift of why he is writing. This study guide is structured with Romans 14–16 first just to help correct the malpractice of ignoring those chapters! Romans has an abundance of questions and answers which will be highlighted in the study guide. If chapters 1–11 concern redemption, chapters 12–16 concern peace, so the two major words for this study guide are "redemptive peace." Redemption without the peace of chapters fourteen and fifteen misreads Romans, but so does peace without the redemption of the lengthy chapters preceding chapter fourteen.

I believe Romans 1–4 and 9–11 are the residue of Paul's engagements with those who opposed his mission to the gentiles. Most importantly, Paul experienced heat everywhere he planted churches because he did not require gentiles to follow the law of Moses. Romans 1–4 and 9–11 record how he learned to respond to his critics. Chapters 5–8, then, are his "theory" of how best to live the Christian life apart from a traditional observance of the laws of Moses.

The best way to read Romans is to start near the back, with the complicated problems in Romans 14–15. That's what we will do.

WORKS CITED IN THE STUDY GUIDE

(Throughout the Guide you will find the author's name and title as noted in this book listing with page numbers whenever I cite something from it):

Michael J. Gorman, *Romans: A Theological and Pastoral Commentary* (Grand Rapids: Wm. B. Eerdmans, 2022). [Gorman, *Romans*]

A. Katherine Grieb, *The Story of Romans: A Narrative Defense of God's Righteousness* (Louisville: Westminster John Knox, 2002). [Grieb, *Romans*]

Thomas L. Hoyt, Jr., "Romans," in *True to Our Native Land: An African American New Testament Commentary* (ed. Brian Blount, et al.; Minneapolis: Fortress, 2007). [Hoyt, "Romans"]

Sarah Heaner Lancaster, *Romans* (Belief: A Theological Commentary on the Bible; Louisville: Westminster John Knox, 2015). [Lancaster, *Romans*]

Richard N. Longenecker, *The Epistle to the Romans* (Grand Rapids: Wm. B. Eerdmans, 2016). [Longenecker, *Romans*]

Scot McKnight, Joseph A. Modica, eds., *Preaching Romans: Four Perspectives* (Grand Rapids: Wm. B. Eerdmans, 2019). [McKnight-Modica, *Preaching Romans*]

Scot McKnight, B.J. Oropeza, *Perspectives on Paul: Five Views* (Grand Rapids: Baker Academic, 2020). [McKnight-Oropeza, *Perspectives on Paul*]

Scot McKnight, Lisa Bowens, Joseph A. Modica, *Romans in the Pew* (forthcoming, 2023). [McKnight,Bowens, Modica, *Romans in the Pew*]

Scot McKnight, *Reading Romans Backwards: A Gospel of Peace in the Midst of Empire* (Waco, Texas: Baylor University Press, 2019). [McKnight, *Reading Romans Backwards*]

Becky Castle Miller, *Teaching Romans Backwards: A Study Guide to* Reading Romans Backwards (Waco, Texas: Baylor University Press/1845 Books, 2019). [Miller, *Teaching Romans Backwards*]

N.T. Wright, "The Letter to the Romans," in *The New Interpreter's Bible*, vol. 10 (Nashville: Abingdon, 2002), 393–770. [Wright, "Romans"]

REDEMPTIVE PEACE CHALLENGED BY AMBITION

Romans 14:1–12

Special Note to the Reader: We begin with Romans 14–16 because these chapters provide graphic information about the tensions among believers in Rome's house churches. Knowing who is who and who says what clarifies why Paul wrote this letter. Beginning here introduces us to the problems that the entire letter to the Romans will resolve. The Romans themselves were living in this tension. When they heard Paul's letter read to them, they knew what he was saying and to whom he was saying it. And they may have thought Paul was nothing if not a little bold in what he said about them in Romans 14–16.

The problem among believers in Rome, both behind closed doors and whenever they gathered, was ambition. No church is in complete harmony. If it is, give it some time and tensions will arise. Some disharmonies threaten the unity of the church. Some only irritate and get under the skin. Ambition in the USA today mostly points at a desire by many to succeed, and most of us don't see anything wrong with reasonable ambition. But America turned the word "ambition" from an almost entirely negative word into a positive description. How so? Let me explain, because ambition, like ours, gets to the heart of what was going on with believers in Rome.

For most of its history, ambition was seen as rebellion against the order, against one's location or status in one's community and, whether aggressive or not, the attempt to climb and claw one's way up the social ladder. It is at the heart of a desire for greatness, for fame, for celebrity. Since most societies in the ancient world—Jewish, Greek, Roman—were status driven, and one knew one's location, ambition was rage against the system. Of course, the well-heeled were driven by an acceptable ambition of rising to a level of social honor. Until the aggressions were deemed unacceptable. It is a fact of social history that the colonies needed ambition to break free from King George and England, and in so doing gave to the American spirit the virtue of ambition. That spirit continues to drive Americans (King, *Ambition*).

Ambition ruins churches. It can begin well with a passionate Christian committed to a mission of reaching others, or of pressing for a theological vision, or of pushing for a seeker-friendly or liturgical or expository sermon church, or even of one pastor pushing for more leadership. Sometimes the passionate ones are in the right, and sometimes they aren't. The passionate one is usually the one who can't recognize when he has gone over the line from mission passion to controlling ambition. If the ambitious passion takes hold, a church becomes toxic.

[1] Accept the one whose faith is weak, without quarreling over disputable matters. [2] One person's faith allows them to eat anything, but another, whose faith is weak, eats only vegetables. [3] The one who eats everything must not treat with contempt the one who does not, and the one who does not eat everything must not judge the

one who does, for God has accepted them. [4] Who are you to judge someone else's servant? To their own master, servants stand or fall. And they will stand, for the Lord is able to make them stand.

[5] One person considers one day more sacred than another; another considers every day alike. Each of them should be fully convinced in their own mind. [6] Whoever regards one day as special does so to the Lord. Whoever eats meat does so to the Lord, for they give thanks to God; and whoever abstains does so to the Lord and gives thanks to God. [7] For none of us lives for ourselves alone, and none of us dies for ourselves alone. [8] If we live, we live for the Lord; and if we die, we die for the Lord. So, whether we live or die, we belong to the Lord. [9] For this very reason, Christ died and returned to life so that he might be the Lord of both the dead and the living.

[10] You, then, why do you judge your brother or sister? Or why do you treat them with contempt? For we will all stand before God's judgment seat. [11] It is written:

> *"'As surely as I live,' says the Lord,*
> *'every knee will bow before me;*
> *every tongue will acknowledge God.'"*

[12] So then, each of us will give an account of ourselves to God.

Ambition's Factions in Rome

Toxic ambition drove two different groups of Roman Christians. Paul labels them "weak" (14:1) and "strong" (15:1). Both groups lurk behind every sentence from 14:1 to 15:13. And they are behind everything in this letter. In today's reading I will extract what we can know about each group and will postpone discussing Paul's instructions to them for the next two passages, plus another one from Romans 16—and only then can we turn to Romans 1:1. I call this reading Romans "backwards" (McKnight, *Reading Romans Backwards*).

Before reading the next paragraph but after reading this one, please read Romans 14:1–15:13. Make two columns on a sheet of paper, and label the left "Weak" and the right "Strong." As you read, write in each column the characteristics of each group, and for convenience make sure to write chapter and verse. Go ahead. Put down this book, open up your Bible, and see what you find.

Here are my conclusions to which you can compare yours. The two italicized words at the bottom of each column summarize the major themes of that group.

Powerless/The Weak (in faith)	Powerful/The Strong (in faith)
Eats only vegetables (14:2, 14, 20)	Eats anything (14:2, 14, 20)
Judges the strong (14:3, 4, 10)	Shows contempt for weak (14:3, 10)
Observes sacred days (14:5)	Observes no sacred days (14:5)
Abstains from meat (14:6, 14, 20)	Eats meat (14:6, 14, 20)
Fidelity	*Freedom*
Powerless	*Powerful*

We pause briefly to notice that Paul seems to be in the middle of this debate. He almost takes sides, and you may think he actually does.

Paul

Nothing is unclean (14:14, 20)
Personal conviction matters (14:14, 17–18, 22)

It is highly likely that the ones Paul labels as "weak" are Jewish believers and those labeled "strong" are gentile believers. However, it's not simple, because Paul is a Jewish believer who evidently considers himself strong! The concern about food suggests kosher or non-kosher food (14:14, 20). Which means these two columns are as much conviction as they are ethnic. And we should see these labels also as social. In Romans 15:1 Paul will call them the Powerful and the Powerless, in Greek *dunatoi* and *a-dunatoi*. The NIV translates "strong" and "weak," but the terms powerful and powerless have some connotations for us that strong and weak do not. The terms powerful and powerless pertain to status, to one's location on the social status ladder. Gentile believers, who had greater status, were pushing Jewish believers around.

It's an old story: the Powerful and the Powerless. Mesopotamia, Persia, Egypt, Greece, Rome–all lived the stories of the Powerful overwhelming the Powerless. It was Rome's way of life. Paul does not appreciate that this old story has become part of the Christian story.

Now for Ambition

The problem for Paul springs from the ground of ambition, though he does not use this word until Romans 15:20 where it is his (counter cultural) "ambition" to go around the Roman empire gospeling about Jesus. But in his world most uses of the idea of ambition are negative and have to do with aggressive social climbing. Look up the following to catch the odor of (selfish) ambition: Romans 2:8; 2 Corinthians 12:20; Galatians 5:20; Philippians 1:17 and 2:3; James 3:14, 16. Mix into this the more positive sense for the social upper classes of Rome and you find a heady brew of something being acceptable only for the elite and powerful, unacceptable for the powerless *hoi polloi,* and just imagine a few of the Roman Christians having some upper class possibilities and others resenting that . . . and you are not only in Rome but you are probably sitting in a middle row in your own church!

In Rome both the Weak and the Strong, the Powerless and the Powerful, are fueled by some version of selfish ambition. The Weak want to be in control and seen as the top of the heap, and the Strong want to be in control and seen as the top of the heap. The former claimed (biblical) "fidelity" and the latter claimed "freedom." I have inserted these terms into our columns above in italics at the bottom of the lists. We can call them the Fidelity faction and the Freedom faction. Both had a handle on the truth of the gospel, and both exaggerated their claims. Both created factions in the one church of Jesus Christ in Rome. Those in the Freedom faction no doubt, behind closed doors, did some strutting and tut-tutting, while those in the Fidelity faction added "SMH" to their memos to one another.

What Happened?

How did the factions form? Here's the best hypothesis on offer today. The house churches of Rome were founded by Jewish believers, perhaps converted to Jesus at Pentecost. They were growing and making an impact all the way into the inner circles of the emperor Claudius. So provoked was he by his wife Messalina's affair and the negative publicity he got when he married his niece (Agrippina the Younger), not to forget the growth of the churches in Rome, that he made the Jews and Jewish Christians a scapegoat and expelled them from the City of Rome. We read about this in Acts 18:2. Here's the suggestion then: *in the absence of the founding Jewish believers, the gentile believers took over direction in the churches*. Their freedom theology was no longer a faction but the rule, and they became the Powerful.

Exiles often return. The Jewish believers did. When they got back home, they learned quickly they were no longer as powerful as they imagined. Tension arose and that tension is what best explains the ambition battles among the believers in Rome.

Why begin here?

My father was an English teacher, and he taught my sisters and me never to judge a book by its cover nor skip ahead to the end of a book to discover where the plot will lead the reader. But I'm doing that here. Romans is so long, so complex, and so hard to understand at times (especially chapters 9–11), that some drop out before they finish and others, because they never suspected the Weak and Strong tensions, don't incorporate that tension into their readings of Romans 1–11. But once you see the tension between the Powerful and Powerless you can never unsee it. So we begin here to give us a better perspective on the whole letter when we get back to chapter 1.

The redemption both groups had experienced in Christ was in need of the peace that naturally flows from redemption.

Questions for Reflection and Application

1. Why does McKnight begin the study guide near the end, with chapters 14–15?

2. How and why did the word "ambition" shift meanings and connotations? What does this have to do with Romans?

3. Which group does McKnight conclude Paul labels as "Strong"? Which group is "Weak"?

4. How can using the words "Powerful" and "Powerless" instead of "Strong" and "Weak" help us understand better what was going on in the Roman churches?

5. How have you seen ambition impact your own life and the life of your church, in both positive and negative ways?

FOR FURTHER READING

William Casey King, *Ambition: A History from Vice to Virtue* (New Haven: Yale University Press, 2013).

THE UNITY AT THE TABLE OF REDEMPTIVE PEACE

Romans 14:13–23

[13] Therefore let us stop passing judgment on one another. Instead, make up your mind not to put any stumbling block or obstacle in the way of a brother or sister. [14] I am convinced, being fully persuaded in the Lord Jesus, that nothing is unclean in itself. But if anyone regards something as unclean, then for that person it is unclean. [15] If your brother or sister is distressed because of what you eat, you are no longer acting in love. Do not by your eating destroy someone for whom Christ died. [16] Therefore do not let what you know is good be spoken of as evil. [17] For the kingdom of God is not a matter of eating and drinking, but of righteousness, peace and joy in the Holy Spirit, [18] because anyone who serves Christ in this way is pleasing to God and receives human approval.

[19] Let us therefore make every effort to do what leads to peace and to mutual edification. [20] Do not destroy the work of God for the sake of food. All food is clean, but it is wrong for a person to eat anything that causes someone else to stumble. [21] It is better not to eat meat or drink wine or to do anything else that will cause your brother or sister to fall.

[22] *So whatever you believe about these things keep between yourself and God. Blessed is the one who does not condemn himself by what he approves.* [23] *But whoever has doubts is condemned if they eat, because their eating is not from faith; and everything that does not come from faith is sin.*

Hobbits love to eat with one another. It is said they would eat six meals a day if they could. I don't know how many meals the Roman Christians would eat if they could, but they are like hobbits in their love for eating with one another. Unless you were in the other faction. Unless your ambition was splintering relationships. The factions showed up in bright lights in the noticeable seating arrangements at the meals. Paul's message for them is (1) eat together and (2) he had some very good reasons, which form the network of verses in Romans 14–15.

Unity at the Table

The letter of Romans was written to establish a theological foundation for unity at the table. Yes, for many of us Romans is so detailed in theology that we may wear down and drop out at the end of chapter eight, or perhaps after winding our way through chapters nine, ten, and eleven. So many drop out they fail to see the practical dimensions of this letter that begin in chapter twelve. (McKnight, *Reading Romans Backward*).

Three questions can be asked and answered about eating with one another.

WHO'S AT THE TABLE?

We need now to read again Romans 14:1–15:13 and write out what Paul tells the Powerless/Weak and the Powerful/Strong to do (and not to do), what Everyone is to do, and what Paul believes himself. It is not always easy to figure out at times which line belongs with Everyone and which with Paul. That's because what Paul says to Everyone is what he believes! Doing this exercise helps us to fill in the profiles of the two groups among believers in Rome that we began doing in the previous passage. By the time we are done with today's passage, we will have a good profile of each group. We want to keep our focus on the major ideas and so cannot enter into all the details.

Powerless/Weak	Powerful/Strong
	Accept the weak (14:1)
	No quarreling (14:1)
Does not eat everything (14:3)	Eats everything (14:3)
Sacred days (14:5)	Everyday alike (14:5)
	Bear with the weak (15:1)
	Avoid self-pleasing (15:1)

Everyone

Worship and eat to the Lord (14:6)
Live and die for the Lord (14:7–8)
Avoid stumbling blocks (14:13, 15b, 20–21)
Act in love (14:15a)
Pursue peace and edification (14:19)
Preference respected (14:22)

Avoid doubts (14:23)
Please neighbors more than self (15:2)
Unity glorifies God (15:5–6)
Accept one another (15:7)

Paul

People differ (14:2, 13)
Personal conviction matters (14:14, 17–18, 22)
God accepts both sides (14:3–4)
All will be judged (14:10–12)
Nothing is unclean (14:14, 20)
Kingdom is not eating and drinking (14:17)
Kingdom is righteousness, peace, joy (14:17–18)
God's mission to the gentiles (15:8–12)

If one looks at which group receives the most instructions and considers what that says about what is most important, one sees that Paul is easy on the Weak and heavier on the Strong and most of all, he's instructing Everyone. We can follow suit by not focusing on who's good and who's bad but on what we *all should be doing in the way of Christ*. The lines under "Paul" above give a theological basis for what Paul tells Everyone to do, especially the Strong. It can be summarized in one simple order: eat together. Which may strike you as banal. It's not. Beverly Daniel Tatum knows eating with another and not eating with one another are social actions, which is why she wrote her national bestseller, *Why Are All the Black Kids Sitting Together in the Cafeteria? And Other Conversations about Race*. Perhaps Paul's letter could be entitled "Why Are All the Powerful Sitting Together in the Small Group?"

The above lists and the lists in our previous passage can now be put together to gain a profile of the messy situation among Roman believers. This was in Paul's head when he began the letter as well as in the heart and soul of the Romans themselves. After all, this mess was their world, and they were looking at one another as the letter was being read. It helps us to know about the mess before we open chapter one. Before we get there, we can ask a question that will sketch what Paul thinks they should do and this, too, helps us to read the letter when we get back to chapter one.

How Should They Eat Together?

He tells the Strong to "accept the . . . weak" (14:1) and to "bear with the weak" (15:1), and for the first he points out their weak *faith* and for the second he speaks of *failings* (NIV). The Greek of 15:1 has a sharper social edge, and can be translated "We, the Powerful, ought to bear with the *weaknesses* of the Powerless" (15:1). But the big terms for now are "accept" and "bear with." When we combine "accept" with food-and-days concerns in this passage, we know we are looking at typical kosher food regulations and calendar practices of Jewish believers in Jesus.

Instead of making a division at the table, the Strong were to welcome one another and sit next to one another as siblings, as equals. Which is why Paul instructs the Strong not to be quarreling with the Weak over their days and food practices (14:1). Discussions were turning into disputes over discernment, not doctrine. Paul tells the Powerful, again in 15:1, that they were to welcome the Powerless instead of doing what they wanted and demanding their viewpoint. The Strong were "not to please" themselves. Respect for the other required dropping the debates. (Easier said than done.)

The issue deserves our respect—for both sides! Some actions become symbolic of how serious one's commitment is. They mark one as faithful. I will give one example that plays little role in most churches, but it was a marker in my church growing up. Carrying one's Bible, preferably a Scofield Reference Bible, to church and following along in one's own Bible during the sermon. The committed carried the Bible; those who didn't were perceived as not-so-committed. (You can name your church's markers.) So clear was this a marker that we didn't even have pew Bibles. Carrying one's Bible then communicated to many one's commitment to the faith. It didn't really, but it in some ways was how a person communicated to others *I'm all-in*. Such were the food laws and sacred days for the Weak, and just as much were they not for the Strong.

What Are the Basics for Eating with One Another?

By the time Paul writes this letter, he's a veteran missionary. He's got in his memory a storehouse of stories and lessons learned. One compartment in his brain was a big one: there will nearly always be tension between gentile believers and Jewish believers on how best to live. Some will think the law of Moses matters more than others. From two decades plus of watching this tension grow among his churches, Paul developed some principles to live by. He learned that the table revealed both the presence and the lack of unity among believers. Just as the cafeteria table in a public place, like a school, reveals who's who and who's not. I will look at six major ideas that can re-shape our approach to differences among believers and thus bring a greater sense of unity at the table.

First, we can grow in unity if we learn to respect that people differ on some issues. Paul sees this as a matter of personal conviction and faith. He knows the Powerless can go to Leviticus, but he knows, too, the Powerful will appeal to other Scriptures. Notice how he puts it when he writes "One person's faith allows them to eat anything, but another . . ." (14:2). Yet, Paul wants each person's preferences on such matters to be shaped by a clear faith and conviction (14:23). Paul says his own conviction (or preference) is that nothing is unclean (14:14), and he knows that different people can serve God either way (14:17–18). He sounds uber modern when he writes "whatever you believe about these things keep between yourself and God" (14:22).

Second, we can eat together in unity if we keep in mind that God accepts both the Powerless and the Powerful, not one or the other. Here are stunning words about the two sides: "God has accepted them" (14:3). Let each person, he teaches, worship and live and even die before the Lord (14:6–8). We are only a toenail from crossing the line into the implied conclusion: *If God has accepted them, we should too!*

Third, we can achieve unity if we keep in mind that God (not we) will be the final judge in these matters (14:10–12). The judging actions of both sides are in view in Paul's words. Notice "judge" in 14:10 and 14:3, and then "treat with contempt" in the same verses. Both are warned that God, not they, are the final judge. And, if we need the reminder, which we sometimes do, "God has accepted them" (14:3).

Fourth, Paul's mission is to the gentiles, and in his gentile mission he has learned that food laws and sacred days can divide Christians deeply. We can live into a deeper unity if we strive for what is ultimately final. One of Paul's own theological conclusions is that "nothing is unclean it itself," and about this he is "full persuaded in the Lord Jesus" (14:14). He says later "all food is clean" (14:20). This means kosher food practices are fine, but they are not final. Some may choose not to eat pork, but not eating pork is not a mandated choice for all. Paul tolerates differences between Christians on some matters, but those differences are not to divide the believers because they don't matter as much as our unity in Christ.

Fifth, we can reorient all of our behavior around the kingdom in a way that diminishes the significance of acts of symbolic power that become "lines not to cross" between believers. Some may think kosher food is for all, but the kingdom of God is more important. In fact, the kingdom "is not a matter of eating or drinking" but instead all about "righteousness, peace and joy" (14:17). We can eat together in unity, then, if we recognize that the food is not the ultimate good for the kingdom.

Finally, Paul's words to everyone deepen our capacities to achieve unity at the table. Here are some of his wise instructions: avoid causing other believers to fall away from the faith by doing something that totally trips them up. This is not the same as differing from one another. We will not reach total unanimity until the final kingdom, but we can learn not to do things that cause others to lose the faith (14:13, 15b, 20–21). We can pursue peace and love and building one another up in the faith (14:15, 19).

We know real people in our churches, and Paul opens some doors in our next passage to meet some real people in the house churches in Rome. You may be quite surprised what you find.

Questions for Reflection and Application

1. What do Paul's instructions to those at the table tell you about Paul's beliefs and values?

2. Which Jewish traditions and regulations lie behind the conflicts here?

3. How does Paul allow for varying convictions among faithful believers?

4. What are his instructions for unity in the face of difference?

5. What are some of your church's markers that distinguish culturally between the committed and the not-so-committed?

FOR FURTHER READING

Beverly Daniel Tatum. *Why Are All the Black Kids Sitting Together in the Cafeteria? And Other Conversations about Race* (rev. ed.; New York: Basic Books, 2017)

REDEMPTIVE PEACE HOUSEHOLDS

Romans 16:1–16

[1] I commend to you our sister Phoebe, a deacon of the church in Cenchreae. [2] I ask you to receive her in the Lord in a way worthy of his people and to give her any help she may need from you, for she has been the benefactor of many people, including me.

[3] Greet Priscilla and Aquila, my co-workers in Christ Jesus.

[4] They risked their lives for me. Not only I but all the churches of the Gentiles are grateful to them.

[5] Greet also the church that meets at their house.

Greet my dear friend Epenetus, who was the first convert to Christ in the province of Asia.

[6] Greet Mary, who worked very hard for you.

[7] Greet Andronicus and Junia, my fellow Jews who have been in prison with me. They are outstanding among the apostles, and they were in Christ before I was.

[8] Greet Ampliatus, my dear friend in the Lord.

[9] Greet Urbanus, our co-worker in Christ, and my dear friend Stachys.

[10] Greet Apelles, whose fidelity to Christ has stood the test.

Greet those who belong to the household of Aristobulus.

[11] Greet Herodion, my fellow Jew.

Greet those in the household of Narcissus who are in the Lord.

[12] Greet Tryphena and Tryphosa, those women who work hard in the Lord.

Greet my dear friend Persis, another woman who has worked very hard in the Lord.

[13] Greet Rufus, chosen in the Lord, and his mother, who has been a mother to me, too.

[14] Greet Asyncritus, Phlegon, Hermes, Patrobas, Hermas and the other brothers and sisters with them.

[15] Greet Philologus, Julia, Nereus and his sister, and Olympas and all the Lord's people who are with them.

[16] Greet one another with a holy kiss. All the churches of Christ send greetings.

In no other letter Paul wrote does he mention so many names. Romans 16 stands taller than others in introducing to its readers and hearers the people involved. Because we know where at least some of the Jewish synagogues were, and because we know the Christians in this last chapter were on the lower end of the social scale, we also have more than a good idea where these Christians were living. Running north to south through Rome is the Tiber River. Rome's power heart was the Forum, and west of the Forum is an area beyond the Tiber called (today) Trastevere (trast-EH-ver-eh). In the Trastevere many of Rome's poor, including Christians, lived in difficult conditions with constant foul odors. Also snaking through Rome is the Appian Way, and along this road–southeast of the Forum–was another location for Christians. It is likely, too, that some Christians lived in the Aventine (south of the Forum) and off Mars Field (northwest from the Forum) on the Via Lata/Flamina.

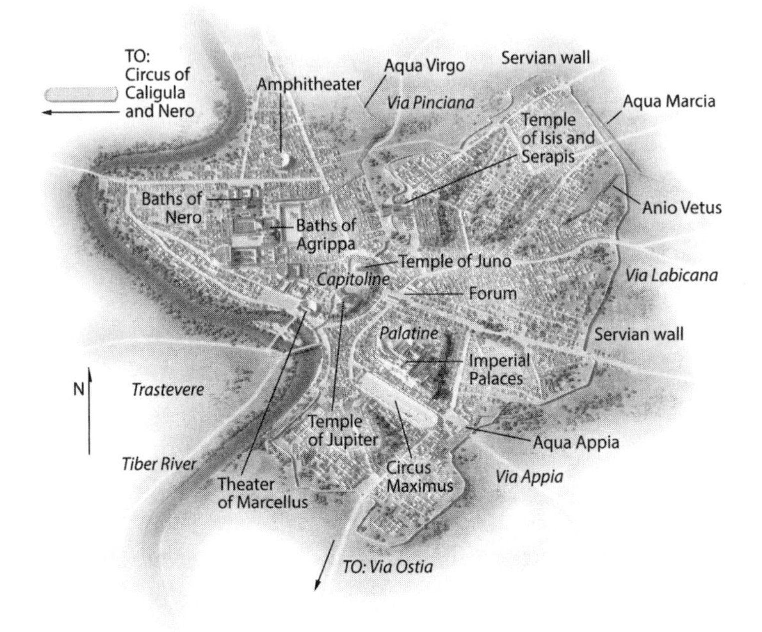

The Benefactor

Always pay attention to who is mentioned first in a list of names. Coming first in Romans 16 is a gentile believer named Phoebe, from the port area near Corinth called Cenchreae. She's a "deacon," and it is inaccurate and diminishing to translate it "deaconess," a term that often refers to women who clean up church kitchens after communion. She's a deacon because she is a leading servant in the church. We need to connect her to Acts 6's original choice of deacons and to the list of character traits of deacons in 1 Timothy 3:8–10, as well as to Philippians 1:1. Phoebe is a leader in her church, which may well meet in her home as she is wealthy enough to be a "benefactor" for Paul and his mission (16:1–2).

This spot in a letter, again at the top of the list of names, is reserved for the courier of a letter. Paul gave Phoebe the letter to deliver to the house churches in Rome. She also probably read the letter aloud to each of the house churches in Rome. Ever read Romans aloud? In front of people? In front of people who could ask questions? Even questions about Romans 7 and 9–11?! Phoebe would have been prepped by Paul on how to read each line, which words to emphasize, and when to slow down and when to speed up as well as which gestures to use. Plus, what to say when they ask about this or that. She's highly respected, and Paul instructs the Romans to "receive her in the Lord" that is not only welcoming but "worthy of his people." Also, they are to provide what she needs in her stay there and return trip.

Just to make this letter real, imagine, as you are reading it, listening to a woman's voice. Imagine when she would pause and what words she would emphasize and soften on. You have to do this aloud, so go somewhere alone and just try it. It opens a door on this most important letter in earliest Christianity.

The House Churches

In Romans 16's list of names, five different households are named: (1) Prisca (NIV has Priscilla) and Aquila (16:3–5), (2) Aristobulus (16:10), (3) Narcissus (16:11), (4) Asyncritus and others (16:14), and (5) Philologus, Julia, and others (16:15). There may be other house churches, but the way each of these is mentioned suggests a separate residence. We don't know if the other names mentioned dwell in one of these households nor if they have their own house churches, but five house churches is a safe conclusion.

It is not uncommon at this point in a discussion to estimate the number of believers living in Rome, perhaps something like 100–200. The size of a church does not its character determine. Ambition breaks through in small house churches and in massive megachurches. Small churches also don't guarantee unity. One can guess that the Powerful gathered in some of these houses and the Powerless in the others. No doubt, there would have been differences in the size and accoutrements of each house. In which case, Paul instructs the Powerful to write up some invitations to the Powerless to come to dinner.

The Demographics

Now some fun. The names mentioned combine those whom Paul knows and those who are leaders, though distinguishing one from the other is not possible from what Paul tells us here. Every name that can be found in ancient Rome has been examined—on inscriptions, and monuments, and letters. Here are some basics from what we find in this list of names:

Jewish names: Mary, Andronicus, Junia, Aquila, probably Prisca/Priscilla, Herodion, Rufus and his mom (cf. Mark 15:21).
Latin names: Ampliatus, Julia, Urbanus.

The Jewish names could be converts from the synagogues and the Latin names for gentile believers from Rome itself. It is quite possible that, on the basis of name alone, both Aristobulus and Narcissus were slaves, and others think Ampliatus, Asyncritus, Julia, Nereus, and his sister were also slaves.

Noticeably, women are prominent in Paul's listing. Here are those with female names: Prisca, Mary, Junia, Tryphaena, Tryphosa, Persis, Rufus' mom, Julia, Nereus' sister, as well as the sisters in Asyncritus' household. It is a fact in the church, not to ignore human history itself, that women are ignored and even silenced. Two recent historians have sorted through and catalogued the stories of hundreds of (almost) silenced female Bible interpreters (Schroeder and Taylor, *Voices Long Silenced*). Most readers of Romans 16 don't even recognize some (or most) of these names as women. Translations would do well to call attention to their names somehow (as I have done in my forthcoming translation of the New Testament called *The Second Testament*). Why not underline the names of women in your Bible.

Prisca and her husband . . . notice the order . . . a woman named first probably indicates that she's got higher status in society or in the church or probably both. They are Paul's mission-sent friends (cf. Acts 18:1–3, 24–26). Junia was later changed from a woman's name to a man's name, Junias, and this non-existent Junias became the name in most Bibles. One can only hope the reason was not because she was a woman with influence and leadership. But that's hope against hope because her name was changed to a man's name because many were uncomfortable because the term "apostle" was connected to her (McKnight, *Blue Parakeet*, 289–305). An early father said she was an "outstanding" apostle and not simply a woman held in high regard by apostles (16:7).

Paul's descriptions of what these women were doing in Rome include deacon-ing and providing (16:1–2); one was a co-worker who risked her life for Paul (16:3), another worked hard for the believers in Rome (16:6), another was imprisoned and an apostle (16:7), some others were hard workers (16:12), and one had mothered Paul (16:13). The women in the Pauline mission that extended to Rome were industrious gospel agents. We must envision these named women as leaders in the house churches.

If you're looking for diversity, this list can guide you to some churches in the City of Rome marked by that diversity. No wonder ambition was set loose, and tensions were at work between the groups. It's one thing for Paul to say we are one in Christ (Galatians 3:28; Colossians 3:11). It's entirely another matter to achieve unity. Paul wrote this letter to offer a vision of peace in the churches setting up shop in the empire's major city, Rome.

Peace begins at an inclusive table. We turn back now to the beginning of this letter with this messy situation among Roman believers in mind. Remember this: when these Romans heard Phoebe read the letter, they were listening in house churches that very well may have been in serious tension with one another.

Questions for Reflection and Application

1. What can historical and cultural context teach us about Phoebe?

2. What surprises you most about the demographic and background information for the Roman house churches?

3. What is notable about the inclusion of so many women in the list of names?

4. Try reading a portion of Romans aloud and imagine how Phoebe might have done it. What insights do you gain from this experience?

5. After having looked at Romans 14–16, what is your understanding of the situation Paul is responding to in the rest of his letter?

FOR FURTHER READING

Scot McKnight, *The Blue Parakeet* (2d ed.; Grand Rapids: Zondervan, 2018).

Joy A. Schroeder, Marion Ann Taylor, *Voices Long Silenced* (Louisville: Westminster John Knox, 2022).

THE GOSPEL MISSION OF REDEMPTIVE PEACE

Romans 1:1–7

Special Note to the Reader: I have put words in bold type about the gospel in today's passage, and the rest concerns the *mission of God* to extend the gospel to all people. These are the two words that matter most in this passage: gospel and mission. (We will discuss "grace" at Romans 3:24.)

[1] Paul, a servant of Christ Jesus, called to be an apostle and set apart for the ***gospel of God—[2] the gospel he promised beforehand through his prophets in the Holy Scriptures [3] regarding his Son, who as to his earthly life was a descendant of David, [4] and who through the Spirit of holiness was appointed the Son of God in power by his resurrection from the dead: Jesus Christ our Lord.*** *[5] Through him we received grace and apostleship to call all the Gentiles to the obedience that comes from faith for his name's sake. [6] And you also are among those Gentiles who are called to belong to Jesus Christ.*

[7] To all in Rome who are loved by God and called to be his holy people:

Grace and peace to you from
God our Father and from the Lord Jesus Christ.

Gospel

The gospel of the earliest apostles, even before Paul, is defined in 1 Corinthians 15:1–28. The uniform gospel in the earliest churches can be found in vv. 3–5, which reads:

> For what I received I passed on to you as of first importance: that Christ died for our sins according to the Scriptures, that he was buried, that he was raised on the third day according to the Scriptures, and that he appeared to Cephas, and then to the Twelve.

That gospel is reduced in 2 Timothy 2:8 to these words: "Remember Jesus Christ, raised from the dead, descended from David. This is my gospel." The gospel of the apostles is found also in the sermons of the Book of Acts.[1] That gospel can be reduced to one word—Jesus—or three words—Jesus is Lord, or Jesus is raised–or to a simple statement: the story of Israel is fulfilled in the story of Jesus, the Messiah, King, Son of God, Savior, and Lord over all.

Now we can see Romans 1:1–7's bold words for what they are: gospel. First, it is *God's* gospel and not Rome's and not the emperor's and not Paul's, and not even the apostles'. It's God's and God's alone. Second, this gospel had *a long build up in history,* a bit like Tolkien's storied plot in *The Lord of the Rings,* where it was promised and awaited and then fulfilled. Third, the gospel's content is a gospel "*regarding his Son* . . . descendant of David . . . Son of God in power by his resurrection" about "Jesus Christ our Lord." Fourth, in these opening words in Romans 1 we must take a good, hard look at the absence of Jesus' atoning death and at the presence of the resurrection as *the moment when the magic of redemption occurs.* Not that Paul devalues the cross, for this is the man who can preach "Christ crucified" (1 Corinthians 1:23). No, not at all. But we are in need of more resurrection in our gospel, and these words show the way. The resurrection snapped the powers of death and sin and systemic evil and launched new creation. That redemption is the benefit of the life, death, resurrection, and ascension of Jesus. The dead man on the cross became the Lord on the Throne because of the ascension (see Nordling and Miller, "Ascension").

I have more than once complained about the Four Spiritual Laws and The Bridge Illustration that focus exclusively on Jesus as an agent of our redemption. The gospel of Romans 1 is a *gospel about Jesus,* about his life, death, burial, resurrection, and ascension and *rule as Lord over all.* The gospel here is one that tells the whole story of Jesus and not just a Good Friday story (McKnight, *King Jesus Gospel*). The four Gospels are called gospels because they tell the story of Jesus, and that is because the story about Jesus is the gospel!

Mission

The God of this gospel about Jesus called the apostle Paul out of one life into another. His second life was a mission to offer the gospel about Jesus to the gentiles. Not by eliminating Jews but by expanding the people of God to include gentiles and Jews on equal footing before God (Romans 11:11–32; 15:8–13). Paul became an "apostle," one sent, God's commissioner to the gentiles throughout the Roman empire.

That mission required Paul to summon gentiles "to the obedience that comes from faith." The quoted words are a common Pauline mouthful! It can mean an obedient kind of faith, or a faith kind of obedience, or the kind of obedience that begins in faith. Paul could have been explicit had he wanted to, but the man prefers dense expressions that can unfold in various directions. The proper response to the gospel Paul preached about Jesus was surrender, that is, trusting in Jesus and surrendering one's life to him in total allegiance and obedience—hence, the obedience of faith or that comes from faith (Bates, *Salvation by Allegiance Alone*). Faith that does not become obedience is not what Paul even means by faith. If you are with me, think about it this way: Paul may well have in mind the division in those house churches. An obedient faith is one that welcomes all those in Christ to the table, and thus works toward peace and unity among believers.

One more word.

Letter

This study guide is about Romans, and Romans is a letter, a very, very long letter. And it's intricate and difficult at times. But they didn't have phones and they didn't have airplanes, and the best way to communicate at times was with well-prepared letters. Paul's letter to the Romans looks, apart from its length, like other letters. We would have heard it read with the author first, the addressees and a greeting. Paul begins with the author of the letter as we would expect (even if he expands that part of the opening for some six verses). He tells us that he, Paul, the one with the gospel mission to the gentiles, is a *slave* of Jesus Christ (NIV has "servant"), he has been sent out by God, and he is set apart by God for this very mission. Paul was *designed by God for this gentile mission.*

After identifying the writer, a letter named the addressees and then greeted the addressees. Paul does both of these in 1:7. He writes this letter to "all in Rome who are loved by God and called to be his holy people." The words just quoted were commonly used in the Old Testament for Israel but are now used for the church. Again, not to replace Israel but to expand them around the Lord Jesus. His greetings become a formula for him: "Grace and peace to you from God our

Father and the Lord Jesus Christ" (1:7). A common enough greeting with a Christian twist, but that twist meant calling Jesus the "Lord," and that was the term for the Roman emperor. Paul knows what he's doing.

Questions for Reflection and Application

1. What is the gospel, according to the New Testament writings?

2. What was Paul's mission?

3. Which features of ancient letters are seen in Paul's letter to the Romans?

4. How did Paul's work serve God's goal of uniting Jew and gentile, and how is that theme evident in Romans so far?

5. In what ways are the words "gospel" and "mission" important in your life?

FOR FURTHER READING

Matthew Bates, *Salvation by Allegiance Alone* (Grand Rapids: Baker Academic, 2017).

Scot McKnight, *The King Jesus Gospel* (revised edition; Grand Rapids: Zondervan, 2016).

Cherith Fee Nordling, Becky Castle Miller, "Ascension," in *The Dictionary of Paul and His Letters*, 2d ed.; edited by Scot McKnight, Lynn Cohick, Nijay Gupta (Downers Grove: IVP Academic, 2023).

A MISSION OF REDEMPTIVE PEACE

Romans 1:8–17

[8] First, I thank my God through Jesus Christ for all of you, because your faith is being reported all over the world. [9] God, whom I serve in my spirit in preaching the gospel of his Son, is my witness how constantly I remember you [10] in my prayers at all times; and I pray that now at last by God's will the way may be opened for me to come to you.

[11] I long to see you so that I may impart to you some spiritual gift to make you strong—[12] that is, that you and I may be mutually encouraged by each other's faith. [13] I do not want you to be unaware, brothers and sisters, that I planned many times to come to you (but have been prevented from doing so until now) in order that I might have a harvest among you, just as I have had among the other Gentiles.

[14] I am obligated both to Greeks and Non-Greeks, both to the wise and the foolish. 15 That is why I am so eager to preach the gospel also to you who are in Rome.

[16] For I am not ashamed of the gospel, because it is the power of God that brings salvation to everyone who believes: first to the Jew, then to the Gentile. [17] For in the gospel the righteousness of God is revealed—a righteousness that is by faith from first to last, just as it is written: "The righteous will live by faith."

Some people are born for what they do, or at least it seems to us they were. Like Nelson Mandela, born to end apartheid; or Mary Beard, born to inform us about ancient Rome; or Mr. Rogers, born to communicate the heart of children and to communicate to them the love of God. Paul was born to extend the gospel about Jesus to the gentile world.

Most of us are engaged in many tasks, but at times someone arises with a single mission shaped by a radical commitment. They seem to have been born for one thing. Most of us are born for several or many callings. Paul was born for one mission. But that does not mean Paul is the model of the Christian life. He is not, he was not, and should not be. Jesus was and is and always will be. Still, our passage is about Paul's mission. We can learn from those who are born for one mission. At least four elements of that kind of life can be detected in today's reading.

Prayer

In our passage Paul attempts to persuade the Romans that he cares about them deeply. Even though he's never been to Rome, and even if most of the believers are unknown to him, he knows good things about them and he wants them to hear that. A cynic might think he's buttering them up for stronger words in the letter, but a charitable reading leads us to think he wants them first of all to know that he loves them.

Paul thanks God for all believers in Rome, and "all" (1:8) here reminds us of *both* the Powerless and the Powerful in chapters 14 and 15. He loves both sides of the division. That he's thanking God for believers only becomes clear when he says "through Jesus Christ." It is through the work of the gospel's redemption that Paul can thank God for gospel work in Rome. The Greek word translated "thank" is *eucharistō*, and it combines "good" (*eu*) with "grace" (*charis*). Thus, to thank God is to express to God the good graces of someone or some group of people, all the while recognizing that what is "good" is the result of God's transforming grace.

It is encouraging to those of us who read this letter backwards that, though there are tensions and battles among those believers, their "faith is being reported all over the world." Just because a church has some tensions does not mean it is not also effective in some other areas. We live in a world that seems all too ready to demonize a church because its leader was abusive or despise an entire state because it votes for the other political party. Paul knows the conflicts in Rome, and he loves "all" of them nonetheless.

Paul wants them to know how important they are to him by saying "God is my witness" and that he "constantly" remembers them to God (1:9) at "all times" (1:10). All times means in his daily prayers and, as an observant Jew, Paul prayed at three set times each day (evening, morning, and mid-afternoon). In all these times he remembers them. In context this suggests his thanksgivings for them, but surely his prayers also morphed into petitions for them.

Now his love for them expresses his intense desire to be with them. His never having been to Rome is not because he has not wanted to come visit them. No, he says, "now at last" and "by God's will" he has been praying that "the way may be opened" for him finally to get to Rome to worship with them and to offer what his calling has to offer to them.

Planning

People on mission pray and they also plan, so Paul's praying meandered, as our prayers sometimes do, into plotting and planning (1:11–13). What he planned was to do what spiritual gifts are designed to do: exercise them among people for their growth. Paul uses a term ("impart") that suggests distributing and sharing and handing out the apostolic gift on a serving tray. Gifts are not designed to enhance our power or prestige but to empower others by giving them away. Paul was no narcissist on the platform performing for his own celebrity (Beaty, *Celebrities for Jesus*). He was slave of Jesus who lived to empower others. Yet, he knew their gifts would lead to both their and his being "mutually encouraged."

Remember this passage intends to express his love for them so now he tells them that he "planned many times to come" to Rome but in God's providence was "prevented." Again, his desire to get to Rome is to exercise his gift for the expansion of the gospel among gentiles. And, as our letter shows, to get the two groups in Rome to make peace with one another.

Obligation

A noticeable element of people with a mission in life is a sense of duty or obligation to that calling. So strong is that sense of a calling that it means they continually have to say no to other opportunities. In their own right many opportunities are good and wholesome and fun and healthy, and some people can't say no, and hence can sense they are not living up to their own calling. Paul-type persons are aimed in one direction, and they keep their eyes, like one navigating a boat, on the dock. Yes, those with this strong sense of a Godward obligation can get lost in their own ambition. Yes, they can become so laser-focused they become relationally insensitive and, yes, they can let their mission and institution creep up and take over. I suspect some thought of Paul that way, at least at times.

Paul informs the Romans right up front that his mission is both to "Greeks" and to "barbarians" (NIV mistranslates with "non-Greeks"). A barbarian in Paul's world was a person who could not speak Greek well. The term is actually a ridicule of the person who mumbles along with a "bar" here and "bar" there but never quite getting the pronunciation right. He broadens it to say he's obligated also to the "wise" and to the "foolish." If he means by wise and foolish what he wrote to the Corinthians, he's flipping Rome's script again. The wise are on the social scale deemed wise but aren't wise with God, while the foolish are those on the social scale deemed foolish but have found the way of God in the gospel (cf. 1 Corinthians 1:18–31). His mentioning of four groups is another version of what he wrote to the Galatians (3:28: Jew/gentile, slave/free, male/female) and to the Colossians (3:11: gentile/Jew, circumcised/uncircumcised, barbarian/Scythian, slave/free). These are all saying much the same. Paul knew what he was called to do–preach the gospel to the gentiles and Jews.

Nothing would be given the power to interrupt Paul's mission. Of course, one's "mission" can get compulsive and obsessive and even downright inhumane at times if one lets mission distort life. Paul had relationships, he ate and drank and slept and took afternoon siestas and went for long walks, and no doubt took in some local orators in cities like Ephesus and Athens and Corinth. Yes, he probably, too, got lost in some ambition. After all, he's not Jesus. But Paul kept returning to his mission because of his obligation.

Honor

A negative statement, designed to affirm its opposite, the positive, opens up verse sixteen: "I am not ashamed of the gospel" (on gospel, p. 36). Shame is the underbelly of a status-conscious world. In a status-shaped and hierarchical society, a person's identity is determined by one's location on the social ladder. I am an honorable upper-class woman, I am a dishonored male slave. Neither a crucified Jew nor preaching about him as one's life mission are honorable vocations for the way of Rome. For them Paul's devotion was ridiculous and dishonorable, degrading, and shameful. To say he is not ashamed then is to say he is *honored to be called to be an apostle of the Lord Jesus Christ.* Others may discredit him, but he's honored for the very things they discredit him. The heart of the gospel—the mission, the life, and the ethics of Jesus—flips the Roman script. What they considered status-enhancing, the gospel discredits, and what they discredited, the gospel elevates to upper status. As Michael Gorman, whose study of Romans puts one into a safe pair of hands, says it, this claim is an "utterly counterintuitive and countercultural perspective" (Gorman, *Romans,* 66).

This gospel is God's "power that brings salvation" (NIV) or that leads the cosmos toward salvation (Romans 8, a salvation that becomes effective for "everyone who believes.") Here Paul turns back to his mission to all persons but this time with his special twist: "first to the Jew, then to the Gentile" (1:16). The Book of Acts over and over recounts Paul entering a city, heading straight to the synagogue, preaching and gospeling and debating, then getting kicked out, and then finally setting up a church in someone's home where the gospel attracted more and more gentiles. That process is what "first" and "then" mean.

Now we come to a verse pregnant with life! Paul preaches a gospel and "in the gospel the righteousness of God is revealed" (1:17). We can translate "revealed" as "is apocalypsed" to emphasize how utterly transcendent and history-changing this act of God is. Righteousness is a rich and complex term. It refers to God as righteous as well as to God's own covenant faithfulness to his promises to Abraham; it includes God's standard for what is right; it entails Jesus himself being the

One who is altogether right(eous); it leads to God making things right in Jesus Christ; thus, it refers to God's justice and God establishing justice; and it prompts covenant people who follow Jesus being empowered by the Spirit to live the right kind of life in a life of faithfulness (and allegiance to Jesus). God is right and God does what is right—these are the two poles of the expression "righteousness of God." I turn again to a wonderful sentence by Michael Gorman: "God *does* what God *is*: the righteous God acts righteously; the God of justice creates justice; the faithful God practices fidelity; God the savior saves" (Gorman, *Romans*, 69). In the gospel God reveals what makes all things right.

The emphasis in Romans 1:17 is on Jesus being the Right One who, through his death and resurrection (4:25), declares people right and transforms them into the right kind of life. These occur "by faith from first to last" (1:17). This NIV translation more literally could be translated "out of faith, toward faith." In that dense expression we find ourselves in a puzzle, and perhaps Paul wanted it that way. It could mean out of God's faithfulness toward believers' own faithfulness, or out of Jesus' own faithfulness toward believer faithfulness. I prefer one of those first two, but not all agree. Thus, it might mean instead out of the Strong's faith toward the Weak's faith, or from Abraham's faith toward the church's faith, or it might just mean "altogether by faith"! What is clear is that believers only find a right standing with God and a right life before God "by faith."

If Paul's mission ever got distracted it was because he got lost in some discussion about theology, which is what happened to me in these last two verses. His mission was a gospel mission, and it was for all people, and anyone who believed could experience redemption through Jesus Christ.

Questions for Reflection and Application

1. Who is the model of the Christian life, and why does that matter?

2. What are the elements of Paul's prayer?

3. How should spiritual gifts function in a church?

4. What function do obligation and honor play in helping people stay on mission?

5. What were you born to do?

FOR FURTHER READING

Katelyn Beaty, *Celebrities for Jesus: How Personas, Platforms, and Profits are Hurting the Church* (Grand Rapids: Brazos, 2022).

REDEMPTIVE PEACE REJECTS STEREOTYPES

Romans 1:18–32

[18] The wrath of God is being revealed from heaven against all the godlessness and wickedness of people, who suppress the truth by their wickedness, [19] since what may be known about God is plain to them, because God has made it plain to them. [20] For since the creation of the world God's invisible qualities—his eternal power and divine nature—have been clearly seen, being understood from what has been made, so that people are without excuse.

[21] For although they knew God, they neither glorified him as God nor gave thanks to him, but their thinking became futile and their foolish hearts were darkened. [22] Although they claimed to be wise, they became fools [23] and exchanged the glory of the immortal God for images made to look like a mortal human being and birds and animals and reptiles.

[24] Therefore God gave them over in the sinful desires of their hearts to sexual impurity for the degrading of their bodies with one another. [25] They exchanged the truth about God for a lie, and worshiped and served created things rather than the Creator—who is forever praised. Amen.

[26] *Because of this, God gave them over to shameful lusts. Even their women exchanged natural sexual relations for unnatural ones.* [27] *In the same way the men also abandoned natural relations with women and were inflamed with lust for one another. Men committed shameful acts with other men, and received in themselves the due penalty for their error.*

[28] *Furthermore, just as they did not think it worthwhile to retain the knowledge of God, so God gave them over to a depraved mind, so that they do what ought not to be done.* [29] *They have become filled with every kind of wickedness, evil, greed and depravity. They are full of envy, murder, strife, deceit and malice. They are gossips,* [30] *slanderers, God-haters, insolent, arrogant and boastful; they invent ways of doing evil; they disobey their parents;* [31] *they have no understanding, no fidelity, no love, no mercy.* [32] *Although they know God's righteous decree that those who do such things deserve death, they not only continue to do these very things but also approve of those who practice them.*

If you read the title for today's passage, you might be surprised by the wording. Let me explain. Romans 1:18–32, if it actually begins the substance of Paul's long letter to the Romans, is a mighty abrupt and harsh way to open any letter. Bam! God's wrath of judgment is being poured out so look out! That's an unusual, unparalleled opening for Paul. Plus, if Romans 1–3 is Paul's evangelistic message, and 1:18–32 tries to convince gentiles they are sinners, is this Paul's style of doing so? (I doubt it.) And, if chapter two is his attempt to show Jews as sinners, would it work? (Doubtful.) And, perhaps most importantly, why would Paul try to evangelize a group he affirms already as believers (1:7)? This abrupt, harsh opening needs explanation.

Because of chapter divisions we can miss what is the most important line for understanding today's passage. That line opens the next chapter, Romans 2:1:

> You, therefore, have no excuse, you who pass judgment on someone else, for at whatever point you judge another, you are condemning yourself, because you who pass judgment do the same things.

That accusation is just as harsh as 1:18 and perhaps harsher. We need to read them together because only 2:1's harshness explains the harshness of 1:18–32.

Here is what I mean: Paul writes 1:18–32 to incite someone or some group to point long damning fingers at gentile sinfulness. Whoever that person is, he trades in common stereotypes about the all-too-prevalent sins of gentiles. At least that's the stereotyped reputation for gentiles. The someone Paul points at in 2:1 is the someone pointing fingers at stereotyped gentile sinners in 1:18–32. And here's where we can tie the later parts of this letter together with the earlier parts: Paul is pointing at the Powerless's tendency to "judge" the Powerful because they're gentiles, *and we all know how gentiles act* (so the Powerless are saying to one another). Put in sharper, cleaner terms: Romans 2 will appeal to the Powerless (not to the Powerful) to set down their stereotypes of gentiles because the Powerless, too, have their own shortcomings and sins. Romans 1:18–32 then is a set-up, a rhetorical move to get the Powerless's attention, to appeal to their own sense of privilege, and then to lower the boom on them for their wrongdoing. He'll give the Powerful plenty of criticism too.

Think of stereotypes we have of others *until we get to know them*. We hear such language about those who support the other political party. Both *The New York Times* and Fox News use them every day. The newest word on the block is to accuse the other side of being "extremists." We use stereotypes for theological groups: Calvinists don't care about evangelism, Arminians trivialize God. Evangelicals don't care about social justice, mainliners don't care about foreign missions (unless it's social action). Honesty requires that there's always at least a grain of truth that provokes people to turn something about a group or person into an exaggerated stereotype. Yes, gentiles—according to pious Jews—were known for idolatry and sexual indulgence. But, but, but . . . Paul wants one very special "You" to knock it off. He does it by setting them up in 1:18–32 and then turns on that "You's" own sinfulness in chapter two.

Notice what 2:1 says before we explain the rest of chapter one. There is someone named "You" passing "judgment on someone else [those in 1:18–32]." Here is a crucial Bible verse. In Romans 2 Paul uses the term "judge" (*krinō*) seven times in five verses (2:1, 3, 12, 16, 27). Other than God judging humans in Romans 3 (3:4, 6, 7), Paul only uses this term in the rest of the letter in one other chapter: he uses "judge" eight times for the Powerless's judgmentalism in chapter fourteen (14:3, 4, 5, 10, 13, 22). He never uses this term for gentiles in this letter. The Powerful don't "judge." Instead, because they are higher in status, they "treat with contempt" those who are Powerless (14:3, 10). This wandering in terms can get a bit complicated, but Paul goes all complicated in Romans, and we will all have to adjust. Peter, you may recall, said Paul's "letters contain some things that are hard to understand" (2 Peter 3:16). Let's all agree that if Peter had trouble, we will probably have more trouble!

Here are three elements of the stereotype that Paul knows will appeal to the "You" of Romans 2:1.

All Humans Are Accountable to God

God's "wrath," a term very well-known from both the prophets and contemporary Jewish writings, "is being revealed" *right then and there in Rome in what everyone can see* (1:18). He does not say "was revealed" or "will be revealed" but *is*. God exposes "all the godlessness and wickedness of people" because the omniscient God sees it all. God's wrath, as Sarah Lancaster has said, "is not an explosive fit of anger" but is God's "displeasure" and "negative judgment" and "discipline" (Lancaster, *Romans*, 27, 28). Rather, it is God's deeply personal reaction to sinfulness that can ruin a person God has created. Paul wants the "You" of 2:1 to see that God's judgment here concerns humans "who suppress the truth" by a kind of life that gradually makes them incapable of recognizing sin. All humans are held accountable to God because all humans can perceive "God's invisible qualities" on the basis of "what has been made" by God (1:20).

Knowing God—this is the assumption Paul makes in full confidence—these sinners neither gave God glory nor thanks but instead, in their claims to smartness, "exchanged" God's glory for "images" and idols. One prophet after another and one Jewish writing after another mention gentile idols, and every city the archaeologist unearths reveals idols in abundance. Most, if not all, homes in Rome had personal idols in them. A second "exchanged" occurs in 1:25, and this time they discard "the truth about God for a lie," and that lie is idol worship. Google a museum in Ephesus or Athens or Rome, look at their displays, and you will see both the grandeur of gentiles and idol after idol.

As Phoebe reads this letter, she knows every listener, and especially the "You" of 2:1, is nodding the head in agreement. The listeners all agree that by God's own creation one can see that God exists. And the listeners perceive that the height of sin is to turn from a God-ordained-human-knowing-of-God to one's own kind-of-knowing, which turns into self-and idol-worship.

God's Judgment Is a Response to Human Sinfulness

A pattern in Romans 1:24, 25, and 28 pops out to the reader of Romans: "God gave them over." God's judgment *responds to human sin*. Let me be graphic. Some believe each human is born with God standing over them with the sword of judgment, but Paul does not put it that way—ever. As a typical Jew, he knew God's judgment was based on the behavior of humans. These gentiles are idol-worshippers, and they are responsible for suppressing what God gave them by creation to know.

The tragedy of such sin is that humans diminish themselves. God hands them over to sexually degrading their bodies (1:24), to "shameful [sexual] lusts [or desires, passions]" (1:26–27), and to a "depraved mind" (1:28). In response to human sin, God surrenders humans to their own wills–and that's what wrath is. He surrenders humans to such practices in order that they may repent, lament, and convert.

Stereotypes Work until "You" Becomes the Judge

Paul uses twenty-one very typical terms for human sinfulness in three verses alone (1:29–31). And today's passage sounds a lot like the sins one can read in the *Wisdom of Solomon*, an apocryphal book in some editions of the Old Testament. I want to include a couple of the lines from that book to show how similar it is to what Paul is writing here. First, like Paul, this book thinks one's sins are at times the result of God turning humans loose to sin even more. We read "so that [the wicked] might learn that one is punished by the very things by which one sins" (11:16; NRSVue). Second, you can hear echoes of this book in Romans 1 if one considers 13:1 (such persons "were unable from the good things that are seen to know the one who exists, nor did they recognize the artisan while paying heed to his works") and 14:27 ("For the worship of idols . . . is the beginning and cause and end of every evil").

But here is *Wisdom of Solomon*'s ultimate stereotype of gentile sinfulness. In chapter fourteen the author speaks of murdering children in their secret religious practices, "frenzied revels," adultery, "and all that is a raging riot of blood and murder, theft and deceit, corruption, faithlessness, tumult, perjury, confusion over what is good, forgetful of favors, defiling of souls, sexual perversion, disorder in marriages, adultery, and debauchery" (14:22–26). And then he ties it to the worship of idols quoted immediately above. This kind of listing is a common approach by Jewish authors to describe the notorious sins of notorious sinners, that is, of gentiles. Notice, too, the presence of same sex relations, which was also a common Jewish criticism of gentiles because it was proscribed in the Bible and tradition. It's a stereotype. It's what many people thought. But it's an exaggeration, too. Which doesn't matter when one is amped up for some verbal contest. These sins are the notorious sins *from the angle of someone who is Jewish and believes life ought to be lived as they think the Bible teaches it.* These are not the typical sins of the typical person, but the specific sins of a stereotype: the gentile idolater and sexual sinner.

When Paul starts listing sins in Romans 1:29–31, the "You" of 2:1 is raising his hand in worship, muttering, *Finally, someone is telling it like it is.* That "You" has embraced that stereotype so deeply he suspects the same sins of some of the Powerful among the Roman believers. True or not is not the point. This is how to talk about gentile sinfulness. A kind of, *they're all like this, amen?!*

The problem with stereotypes is that the grain of truth calls attention to a problem until it leads to exaggerations, othering one's fellow believers, and degrading others as inferior. That is, until it is wrong and unfair and unjust and divisive. Stereotyping labels people and almost never with accuracy. Caricatures are not accurate. Stereotyping makes us think we are "not like them" and "better than they are." Stereotyping, most importantly, turns us into judging others, and that means we have usurped the role that God and God alone has in this world. One more observation: no one fits a stereotype perfectly. Talking about a stereotype, Dorothy Sayers entitled her book *Are Women Human?* because, well, of stereotypes. She said this: "What is unreasonable and irritating is to assume that all one's tastes and preferences have to be conditioned by the class to which one belongs" (*Are Women Human?*, 131). Amen. Stereotyping, we all need to learn, is a human problem that does no good for humans. It is even worse in the church because it causes divisions that may never heal.

Which is why we have to turn to Romans chapter two to see what Paul will do with this stereotype of gentile idolatry and sinfulness and the You fashioning the stereotypes.

Questions for Reflection and Application

1. What is the big rhetorical move around subverting stereotypes Paul might be doing in this passage?

2. How does 2:1 help us better understand 1:18–32?

3. How do God's wrath and judgment function in this passage?

4. What contextual light does it provide to see the comparison of Paul's list of notorious sins with the list from Wisdom of Solomon?

5. When have you been misunderstood because someone applied a stereotype to you? When have you misunderstood someone else because you stereotyped them?

FOR FURTHER READING

Dorothy Sayers, *Are Women Human? Penetrating, Sensible, and Witty Essays on the Role of Women in Society* (Grand Rapids: Wm. B. Eerdmans, 2005).

REDEMPTIVE PEACE LIVES IN LIGHT OF THE JUDGMENT

Romans 2:1–16

[1] You, therefore, have no excuse, you who pass judgment on someone else, for at whatever point you judge another, you are condemning yourself, because you who pass judgment do the same things. [2] Now we know that God's judgment against those who do such things is based on truth. [3] So when you, a mere human being, pass judgment on them and yet do the same things, do you think you will escape God's judgment? [4] Or do you show contempt for the riches of his kindness, forbearance and patience, not realizing that God's kindness is intended to lead you to repentance?

[5] But because of your stubbornness and your unrepentant heart, you are storing up wrath against yourself for the day of God's wrath, when his righteous judgment will be revealed. [6] God "will repay each person according to what they have done." [7] To those who by persistence in doing good seek glory, honor and immortality, he will give eternal life. [8] But for those who are self-seeking and who reject the truth and follow evil, there will be wrath and anger. [9] There will be trouble and distress for every human being who does evil: first for the Jew, then for the Gentile; [10] but glory, honor and peace

for everyone who does good: first for the Jew, then for the Gentile. [11] *For God does not show favoritism.*

[12] *All who sin apart from the law will also perish apart from the law, and all who sin under the law will be judged by the law.* [13] *For it is not those who hear the law who are righteous in God's sight, but it is those who obey the law who will be declared righteous.* [14] *(Indeed, when Gentiles, who do not have the law, do by nature things required by the law, they are a law for themselves, even though they do not have the law.* [15] *They show that the requirements of the law are written on their hearts, their consciences also bearing witness, and their thoughts sometimes accusing them and at other times even defending them.)* [16] *This will take place on the day when God judges people's secrets through Jesus Christ, as my gospel declares.*

The "You" of 2:1 shocks the reader. Katherine Grieb, knowing the tight connection of Romans 2 to Romans 1, says Romans 2:1–16 "springs a trap" (Grieb, *Romans*, 31). In fact, when Phoebe read this letter and suddenly, no doubt after a pause, turned to those listening and said (and I translate), "Therefore you are without any excuse, O man, anyone who judges." For that person—and it's a singular "you" not a "y'all"—everything was fine with Paul's harsh words in chapter one. But his sudden, out of the blue "You" jolts everyone in the room to sudden attention.

Imagine a preacher talking about some problem in the community or in history or in some other church, and then suddenly pausing, turning her eyes on the congregation, and saying, "You are the problem!" That's what Paul does. It's a stunning rhetorical move.

> The problem is stereotyping Roman gentiles.
> Or, the problem is judgmentalism.
> The solution is that God will judge everyone on the basis of clear evidence.

Our Escape Valve

No doubt, many of us are already prepared to deflect the strong words in Romans 2 by assigning them to some other group or person. Blaming others is a way of upgrading our own standing, and that's exactly what was happening in Rome. Many have read Romans 2 as Paul's attempt to prove Jews are as guilty as gentiles. But Paul's not addressing Jews *per se* but rather Jewish believers whom he labels the "Weak" or the "Powerless." Their claim to privilege is their heritage and election as God's special people: Abraham, Moses, the covenant, David, the prophets, etc. Admit it, they've got good biblical evidence for their claim to privilege. Paul will affirm Jewish privilege to open both Romans 9 and Romans 10.

Think about the all-too-common stereotypes in our world: sexism, racism, classism, education-ism, wealth-ism, good-looks-ism, success-ism, big-house-ism, ecology-ism, and any other -ism you can think of. Any of those -isms map onto that condemning sense of stereotyping others in Romans 1. Paul shreds our stereotyping of -ism people in chapter two.

Turning Judgmentalism inside Out

Paul uses "judge" seven times in chapter two (2:1 [three times], 3, 12, 16, 27). Whoever Phoebe turns to face as she reads this long letter has a habit of judging others. In fact, the one judging may not be one person but a habit or a character, with the judging person being a representative type. In Romans the one judging represents the Powerless, and Paul will turn in chapter three to face the Powerful as well. He's a total egalitarian when it comes to criticism!

Paul has a simple message for the judging person: "you are condemning yourself, because you . . . do the same things" (2:1). But not really. But, yes, really. Jewish "sins" in some ways were not the same as gentile sins—after all, they weren't idolaters and they were not engaged in the same kind of sexual sins as mentioned in Romans 1. But Jewish "sins" are the same, and this is what Paul means when he says "you . . . do the same things." How so? Whether gentile or Jew, any and every sin is a violation of God's will revealed in the law of Moses (2:12–16). Paul levels the sinning field: both gentiles and Jews, both the Powerful and the Powerless, are sinners who can be redeemed by Christ (3:21--26) by faith (4:1–25) and live the life God wants in the power of the Spirit (5–8).

When Paul speaks in Romans of Jew and gentile, or of the Strong and Weak, he describes more than one's ethnicity. Notice that he speaks of gentiles, or at times of Greeks and even barbarians, and not just Romans or Italians. These terms are more than ethnic groups. These are the labels used in the social profiling of a group of people. The Jews are not only an ethnic group from Judea, but they are also a status, mostly low at that, in the Roman social profiling system. Paul wants to knock people off their perches, to be sure, but their perch is more than ethnicity. Their ethnicity got mixed in with status to become social profiling. Stereotype, then, becomes a very useful word for reading Romans.

Questions Get Their Attention

Read Romans 2–4 carefully and somehow mark each question. (It's okay to write in your Bible!) Phoebe had been instructed by Paul and his co-workers how to read Romans effectively. When she asked a question, she did not then rush to the next word. No, when she asked a question, she paused. The audiences in Rome were not sitting there the way many of us do on Sunday mornings. Half asleep, barely catching the reading of Scripture. As she read the letter, a question asked meant an answer expressed. So, Phoebe would have heard answers and comments and questions back to her. Try answering each question aloud as you read this chapter, pausing to think about what you would have said. Here are the questions asked in this chapter; the first two are in our passage and the others are from tomorrow's passage:

> So when you, a mere human being, pass judgment on them and yet do the same things, do you think you will escape God's judgment?
> Or do you show contempt for the riches of his kindness, forbearance and patience, not realizing that God's kindness is intended to lead you to repentance?
> You, then, who teach others, do you not teach yourself?
> You who preach against stealing, do you steal?
> You who say that people should not commit adultery, do you commit adultery?
> You who abhor idols, do you rob temples?
> You who boast in the law, do you dishonor God by breaking the law?
> So then, if those who are not circumcised keep the law's requirements, will they not be regarded as though they were circumcised?

Romans 1–4 is zipped up tight with questions. There are so many they become uncomfortable. Some no doubt thought, *C'mon Paul, enough with the questions*. More importantly, answering Paul's questions cornered them and corners us in our judgmentalisms. You might think Paul is annoying. (I know I do at times. *Get on with it,* I mutter.) Annoying or not, he gets our attention with these questions.

God's Criterion for the Judgment

His questions lead to these three statements:

God alone is the Judge.
God alone will judge.
God is fair.

A biblical faith learns to live on the basis of God's grace but also learns to face the final, future judgment by God. Not with fear, not with insecurity, but with eyes wide open to the searching truths of God.

Returning back to Romans 1, Paul says the day of judgment is the day of God's "wrath" when God's "righteous judgment will be revealed" (2:5; cf. 1:18). Quoting either Psalm 62:12 or Proverbs 24:12, we hear the criterion for judgment: "God 'will repay each person according to" to their works[1] (Romans 2:6). I learned this long ago that we are saved by faith, but we are judged by works, because our works indicate our faith and express our character. Our works "bear testimony to the depths of a person's character and show whether their relation to God is fundamentally one of faith or unbelief" (Travis, *Christ and the Judgement of God*, 95). Every judgment scene in the Bible, like Matthew 25:31–46, describes God's judgment of humans on the basis of works.

Those who receive God's grace truly become agents of grace. Those who are justified by God are transformed into agents of justice. Those who are liberated by God's grace become agents of liberation. Grace, justification, and liberation are God's transforming powers at work in us. These are the reasons Paul can say we can be justified by *faith* but judged by *works*. They are not polar opposites, but one would not be visible without the other.

There are two results in God's judgment: eternal life (2:7) for those who do what is right, and "wrath and anger" as well as "trouble and distress" for those who don't (2:8–9). With his watchful eye ever on God's covenant with his fellow Jews, Paul adds "first for the Jew, then for the Gentile" (2:9–10). Not even the Jew's very special covenant relation determines the outcome in the final judgment: "God does not show favoritism" (2:11).

When Paul quotes the Old Testament in 2:6 he uses "works" but in this passage he uses other terms as well. Notice these terms for the criterion of God's judgment: "good works" (2:7, where NIV has "doing good") and "working the good" (2:10, NIV has "does good"). The opposite of good works is "self-seeking" and "reject the truth" and "follow evil" (2:8, 9). These general terms suddenly shift at 2:12. Paul shifts from language about good works to the "law." His shift is more than a shift. He stuns the Powerless because Paul believes the essence of the law of Moses has been implanted in the heart of every human being. Some follow the implanted gift and some don't. Those who do actually obey the law in the heart, and those who don't actually disobey the law. So, those who grew up with the law and heard it have no advantage over those who never heard it. What matters is not possessing the law but doing God's will that has been revealed in the law and in every human heart (2:12–15). Again, God will judge "people's secrets [or "hidden, non-public actions"] through Jesus Christ" (2:16).

We, Too

Let's back up to what we observed in Romans 14–15, where the basic instruction was, *Welcome one another*. Remember, welcoming one another formed the presenting problem and the far goal of this letter. We learned this above when we discussed Romans 14–15. Paul has turned to the Judge of 2:1 to reveal that he is no better than the gentile pagan idolater and sexual sinner. He, too, has broken God's law. In fact, the Judge of 2:1 is being summoned to examine his own life to see if he is doing what God wants rather than asserting his superiority to those whom he has stereotyped. Instead of a "You, too" we might turn this into "We, too." In every stereotyping that we use lurks the person who is not doing God's will, and we need to be reminded of this just as the Powerless needed it (and the Powerful, too). We need to be reminded that God alone is the Judge. God alone will judge. God is fair.

We, too, will stand before that God someday. When we learn to live with our eyes on the Father's eyes, we will embrace all the Father's children—Powerful, Powerless—and we will practice peace with one another as those who have been redeemed alongside one another by the same Lord and Savior of us all.

Questions for Reflection and Application

1. How does Paul level the playing field here between Powerful and Powerless?

2. How does Paul push back against social profiling and stereotyping?

3. What does it mean to be saved by faith but judged by works?

4. Why do you think we are tempted to judge and blame others?

5. When you look at your life honestly, how does it impact any sense of superiority you might have?

FOR FURTHER READING

Stephen Travis, *Christ and the Judgement of God: The Limits of Divine Retribution in New Testament Thought* (2d edition; Peabody, Mass.: Hendrickson, 2008).

LESSONS LEARNED ABOUT REDEMPTIVE PEACE

Romans 2:17–29

[17] Now you, if you call yourself a Jew; if you rely on the law and boast in God; [18] if you know his will and approve of what is superior because you are instructed by the law; [19] if you are convinced that you are a guide for the blind, a light for those who are in the dark, [20] an instructor of the foolish, a teacher of little children, because you have in the law the embodiment of knowledge and truth—[21] you, then, who teach others, do you not teach yourself? You who preach against stealing, do you steal? [22] You who say that people should not commit adultery, do you commit adultery? You who abhor idols, do you rob temples? [23] You who boast in the law, do you dishonor God by breaking the law? [24] As it is written: "God's name is blasphemed among the Gentiles because of you."

[25] Circumcision has value if you observe the law, but if you break the law, you have become as though you had not been circumcised. [26] So then, if those who are not circumcised keep the law's requirements, will they not be regarded as though they were circumcised? [27] The one who is not circumcised physically and yet obeys

the law will condemn you who, even though you have the written code and circumcision, are a lawbreaker.

[28] *A person is not a Jew who is one only outwardly, nor is circumcision merely outward and physical.* [29] *No, a person is a Jew who is one inwardly; and circumcision is circumcision of the heart, by the Spirit, not by the written code. Such a person's praise is not from other people, but from God.*

Slow readers of Romans 1–4 encounter something dense and intense. Truth be told, the same is true about Romans 9–11. The arguments buckle into one another. The quotations and allusions to the Old Testament flow, like a river delta, in many directions. The unstated assumptions cause us to cry out for clarification. It's like we have been ushered into a room with specialists having a public discussion and debate about a topic we thought we understood. Even specialists on Romans will admit this–well, most of them anyway. Where did all these questions and problems come from? They did not come from a philosophy classroom or from a local synagogue's mikvah (immersion pool) with fellow rabbis kibitzing about Torah. Where then?

Where Paul Learned

Every line in Romans 1–4 emerged from Paul's missionary work and encounters. If you teach students your favorite subject long enough, you hear most of the questions about a topic. Everywhere he went, in every synagogue he preached and persuaded his fellow Jews to believe Jesus of Nazareth was Israel's Messiah, in every public square where he engaged others, in every workshop where he conversed with disciples and unbelievers, and in every late-night discussion with his closest co-workers Paul worked out responses to his students and his challengers. He listened to those disagreeing with him and figured out how to nurture the faith of believers who had questions and how to refute those who opposed his gospel. He got pushback, he got pressed, he got questions, he got challenged, and Paul learned day after day how to talk gospel in the synagogue, in the workshop, in the public square, and in house church conversations.

Pondering Romans 1–4 and 9–11 as the distillation of Paul's discussions with others has helped me understand Romans as much as anything I've learned. (Had he wanted to make it so, Romans could have been ten times longer than it is.) A handful of core lessons from the conversations and debates distilled into his most constant themes. Consider now three of them.

First Lesson: Jewish Privilege

Today's passage reveals someone labeled the Judge (2:1), or the judging person. The Judge represents the Jew(ish believer) who has stereotyped gentile idolaters. Probably the Powerless speaking about the Powerful. Paul's intent for 2:17–29 complements his intent for 2:1–16. If the former passage teaches that we will all be judged on the basis of our works and not because one group has a covenant advantage, Romans 2:17–29 digs deeper to establish that knowing the law of God, as Jewish believers have and do, does not make such a person obedient or superior. Doing God's will matters, whether by the Jew or the gentile. God gave that law to Israel through Moses. God's intent in giving the law to Israel was to transform them from the inside-out, that is, so they would become Spirit-filled, heart-driven lovers of God and others.

Again, imagine Paul sitting in a synagogue, after he has spoken, getting peppered with questions. Some of the common questions appear in Romans 2–4. Over time he was able to anticipate what he would be asked and how best to respond to them. Galatians was his first go round; Romans is his final go round. One of his never-give-in and never-give-up convictions, no matter the question or disagreement, was that *God's election of Israel gave Jews a privilege.*

Paul will return to their privilege in Romans 9:1–4, but in our passage one can find ten privileges:

1. they are "Jews" (the Greek term is *Youdaios,* Judean),
2. they rest in the law of Moses,
3. they boast in (knowing) God,
4. they know God's will,
5. they know what is superior because of the law,
6. they can point to the pathway for those who are blinded to God,
7. they have the light for those in darkness (Isaiah 42:6–7; 49:6),
8. they can instruct the foolish,
9. they teach children—and again
10. they've got God's revealed will, the law.

Paul will never give up one item in this list. Ever. Israel's got an advantage, the privilege of God's covenant with them. Remember, however, that Paul's got the Weak of Romans 14–15 in mind and not ordinary Jews, who would not be listening to Paul nor care what he has to say. He wants Jewish believers to remember that these privileges remain theirs. He has a rhetorical approach to establishing Jewish privilege in the plan of God—questions.

But we can expand Paul's audience. Because there's so much stereotyping going on today by those who think they are privileged, as Michael Gorman has observed, Paul would ask the following questions of modern-day (non-Jewish) Christians too (Gorman, *Romans,* 102). I agree.

Second Lesson: Ask Questions

Having learned never to press against God's election of Israel and thus their privilege, Paul also learned that the best way to present the gospel and open their minds to the way of Jesus involved asking questions. Oh-so like the rabbis. He learned to connect with his fellow discussion partners' heart by asking them questions and letting them talk. In fact, at least some if not most of the questions we are about to list were asked of him, and the responses Paul offers in Romans 2–4 were edited versions of his own answers. So, he now asks their questions for them and gives new and improved answers to them!

We mentioned questions in the previous passage and how Phoebe would have paused. Now we return to six questions in today's passage, but this time we observe how slanted they are:

1. You, then, who teach others, do you not teach yourself?
2. You who preach against stealing, do you steal?
3. You who say that people should not commit adultery, do you commit adultery?
4. You who abhor idols, do you rob temples?
5. You who boast in the law, do you dishonor God by breaking the law?
6. So then, if those who are not circumcised keep the law's requirements, will they not be regarded as though they were circumcised?

These are questions with a hook, a barb, a pull, and a yank in each. The answers all appear open-ended, but if you answer each one with a *Yes* you're either deceived or perfect.

At the very least the answer to the fifth question (from 2:23) is Yes. If so, and Yes is the only right response, the Judge is a sinner just like the gentile idolaters in Romans 1. He yanks the hook.

Honest answers to each of these five pressing questions, asked to good effect by Phoebe with a long pause for public responses, will lead people to realize that "God's name is blasphemed among the Gentiles because of you," words Paul adapts from Isaiah 52:5 or perhaps from Ezekiel 36:20, 22. In using the words of the prophet(s), Paul creates the image of the Roman believers sitting in a gentile land but, through their failure to observe the law, they have profaned the holy name of God. No indictment could be weightier in the mind of a Jewish believer.

Third Lesson: Observance Is Deeper than Skin

Paul does something in Romans 2:25–27 that twists obedience to law requiring circumcision. He sees observance of that law as either a symbol of the inner life or flat-out hypocrisy. He learned that observance of the circumcision law is deeper than the skin from Moses or Jeremiah (Deuteronomy 10:12–22, more likely Jeremiah 31:31–34). The sacred body and boundary-marking act of circumcision (from Genesis 17) privileges the Jew only if he actually observes the law (Romans 2:25). In fact, if the person fails to observe the law, that man's circumcision dissipates into a hollow symbol. Then Paul digs into the inner life of all humans: if a gentile actually does the will of God, then his non-circumcision counts for circumcision! (2:26–27) I'd love to have been in the room to see the faces of those who wondered aloud if Paul had crossed the line.

Observable Jewishness in Paul's revolutionary interpretation means nothing. Inwardness matters, the heart matters, and the Spirit matters. Each transcends the observable act of circumcision, which when not in the heart turns the law into little more than a "written code" (2:28–29). As Gorman brilliantly says it, "*The heart is the heart of the problem*" (Gorman, *Romans*, 104; all in italics).

Paul has again knocked down a fundamental line in the sand that blocked equal fellowship in the house churches of Rome. Observance does not a Christian make; observance does not a sibling make.

Paul learned these three lessons in his missionary discussions. One lesson after another, one day after another, one discussion after another, one loss of temper after another. His daily discussions drove him into deep prayer, Bible study, and deeper conversations with his co-workers. His mission discussions unearthed senses of privilege that show little differences with the sense of privilege at work in our churches today. We may have privilege (and we white and employed Christians do in the Western world most of the time), but there are some questions for us about how consistent our behavior is with gospel truth, and we always need to be reminded that the observable has value only as it reflects the inner life.

Questions for Reflection and Application

1. How did Paul work out his approach to teaching the gospel by the time he wrote the letter to the Romans?

2. How does God's election of Israel give the Jews privilege?

3. How do Paul's questions manage to prove that the Judge is a sinner?

4. Why are circumcision and other outer markers of belief insufficient to truly prove a person's faith?

5. What outward signs of belief do you practice in your life? How accurate a reflection of your inner life are those practices?

ADVANTAGES IN GOD'S PLAN FOR REDEMPTIVE PEACE: PART ONE

Romans 3:1–8

[1] What advantage, then, is there in being a Jew, or what value is there in circumcision?

[2] Much in every way! First of all, the Jews have been entrusted with the very words of God.

[3] What if some were unfaithful?

Will their unfaithfulness nullify God's faithfulness?

[4] Not at all! Let God be true, and every human being a liar. As it is written:

"So that you may be proved right when you speak and prevail when you judge."

[5] But if our unrighteousness brings out God's righteousness more clearly, what shall we say?

That God is unjust in bringing his wrath on us? *(I am using a human argument.)*

Certainly not!

If that were so, how could God judge the world?

[7] *Someone might argue,* ***"If my falsehood enhances God's truthfulness and so increases his glory, why am I still condemned as a sinner?"***

[8] ***Why not say—as some slanderously claim that we say—"Let us do evil that good may result"?***

Their condemnation is just!

Children who grow up in the church with faithful parents have an advantage in hearing the gospel. If the gospel matters, proximity to the gospel matters. Let's agree with that for the moment. But that proximity does not always lead to a life of following Jesus. Sometimes these children may claim to be Christians, and they may look down on other people who are not Christians, but their discipleship spins into a loose thread. Paul faces a similar situation with the representative Judge of Romans 2, and he chooses a way to educate him and his companions in the fullness of the gospel in Romans 3.

One method of instructing or guiding a discussion is to ask questions. Some of Paul's questions follow up the previous one and others lead to the next question. Paul keeps this passage moving forward with questions, nine of them, and they are listed above with the question itself in bold font. Paul tersely answers each of his questions (in regular font). Some of his own answers are questions themselves (notice 3:6b, 8a). There are more than a few hints of sarcasm in these verses as well. Remember, the Roman Christians, sitting on the floor or standing up or leaning against a wall, pondered each question with their own answers. The experience of hearing this passage read aloud by Phoebe would have been an imposing, intense theological experience. Just try answering each question yourself.

The previous passages were tough on those who claimed the privilege of covenant election, narrowed down in the argument to the law and privilege of circumcision. Privilege did not entitle the privileged to stereotype gentile idolaters. He heard the first question, "What advantage, then, is there . . . ?," on Day One every time he preached in a new synagogue.

Covenant Connection Provides an Advantage

If one of the most symbolic acts of allegiance to God and the law—circumcision—has a deeper-than-skin reality, "What advantage, then, is there in being a Jew?" Which can lead to its twin question, "[What] value is there in circumcision?" (3:1). Paul puts this question into the mouth of the Judge. The question is the Judge's question.

The answer Paul provides in verse two was silently muttered or publicly uttered by every Powerless person in the room. Their answer was "Much in every way!" Then Paul explains why, and I translate what he says next: "First: for they have been entrusted with God's sayings" (3:2). Their privilege begins with the gift God granted them on Mount Sinai—the gift of knowing God's will.

Their and his answers deserve a little more explanation. Paul was asked the Advantage Question many times. In chapter three he gives a brief answer, but he waits until chapter nine for an even fuller answer, which reads:

> Theirs is the adoption to sonship; theirs the divine glory, the covenants, the receiving of the law, the temple worship and the promises. Theirs are the patriarchs, and from them is traced the human ancestry of the Messiah, who is God over all, forever praised! Amen (9:4–5).

Paul stands up for the Powerless. Their emotions calm down. Their advantages and privileges are abundant and clear—and I can't get Rod Stewart's song "Some guys have all the luck" out of my mind. Back to Romans.

The Powerful may be eye-rolling and muttering that Paul is now back-tracking on what he had just said in the previous chapter. If they thought Paul was backing down from the courage of Romans 2, they would be unfair to the apostle. The gift of God comes with the necessity of responding in faithfulness. The Judge was not faithful to God's calling. Possession of the gifts does not redeem the person. Paul both affirms Jewish privilege and then points us right back to the themes of chapter two: God is faithful, humans are not. God calls them to faithfulness.

Let's return to his question that opens chapter three. Is there an advantage for the Jew then? Is there? In 3:9, our next passage, will say "Not at all!" Paul's answer to the question in 3:2's "Much in every way!" was perhaps a bit ironical, if not a tad sarcastic. *Sure they have an advantage, but the real question is, Did they do the will of God?* Privilege promotes stereotyping, both then and today.

God Is Faithful, Humans Are Not

The matter of stereotyping others can help us in how we respond to this text. When we stereotype, or Other others, we set ourselves up as The Judge. Almost no one (I want to be generous) lives up to their own judgments of others. Paul knows this, so he turns now to the stereotypers to reveal their own failures. To get the full force of this text we need to sit next to and with them, as one of them, as Phoebe reads.

When Paul asks questions three and four, he covertly states that the Judge, the stereotyper of stereotypers, was not faithful. "What *if* some [Jews] were not faithful?"–means some were not, which is what he was saying in chapter two.

Such unfaithfulness by them does not erase God's faithfulness. God's faithfulness means God will judge every person—stereotypers included—fairly, justly, transparently, and piercingly.

Paul knocks the walls down when he says, "Let God be true, and *every human* a liar" (3:4). Jew and gentile, Strong and Weak, it does not matter. Human rejection of God or unfaithfulness to God does not nullify God's utter faithfulness to his promise to Abraham. David affirmed the promise, so Paul quotes Psalm 51:4, words perfect for the occasion. A deep conviction of Paul's becomes clear: not all Israel is truly Israel, not all the circumcised are truly circumcised (Romans 9:6–7). Being in Israel and being circumcised require faith and faithfulness, and without them one denies what Israelite and circumcision are designed to accomplish.

We need to pause. God's transforming grace formed a deep and pervasive theme in the whole Bible. Something is off with a pervasively sinful person who claims to be part of God's people. We easily criticize the Judge of chapter two yet fail to see that we, too, are called not just to claim that we have the gift but to surrender our lives to the graces of spiritual growth in the power of the Spirit. Redemption that does not transform fails to be redemptive.

In discussions with his contemporaries, Paul's heard another pushback about God's covenant with Israel seemingly challenged by Jewish unfaithfulness. And it's an odd argument with two layers. One at a time.

> First layer: some contend that God should not blame us if our sinfulness makes God's righteousness brighter, or if our lies bring to the fore God's utter truthfulness. Both glorify God, God gets what God deserves, and *we humans actually help God by being sinful.* Oy! Why not just sin if it leads to something good for God?!

> Second layer: the first layer's odd set of claims has Paul's gospel in mind. His opponents are accusing Paul of his gentile mission bringing into God's people a bunch of gentiles who disregard the law (like the Powerful), and this pollutes the people of God with sin and sinners.

Their foolish logic looks like this then: Stereotyping gentile idolaters by those who are themselves sinning contributes to God's plan of redemption because it enhances God's faithfulness, truthfulness, and glory! Paul counters that logic with this: the Jewish advantage in God's plan does not mean they don't have to be faithful. Faithful covenant people are transformed people.

This passage calls us to watch out for our temptation to stereotype and to remember that we will never live up to the standards we use on others. We can't blame our way out of this one nor can we excuse our way out of it. We need to turn our hearts over to God so God, through the Spirit, can turn us from our judging of others to become agents of grace.

Questions for Reflection and Application

1. Think about the question, "Is there an advantage for the Jew?" How do the different answers to this question ("not at all" versus "much in every way") shape the welcome-one-another concern for Rome?

2. Is God's people polluted by welcoming in groups of sinners?

3. How does God's faithfulness contrast with human unfaithfulness?

4. Why do the Jews who already have covenant advantage still need to be faithful and transformed?

5. Did you grow up Christian? If so, do you feel any sense of privilege because of that faith foundation? If not, how do you perceive the privilege of those who grew up in Christian families?

ADVANTAGES IN GOD'S PLAN FOR REDEMPTIVE PEACE: PART TWO

Romans 3:9–20

[9] *What shall we conclude then?*

Do we have any advantage?

Not at all! For we have already made the charge that Jews and Gentiles alike are all under the power of sin. [10] *As it is written:*

> *"There is no one righteous, not even one;*
> [11] *there is no one who understands;*
> *there is no one who seeks God.*
> [12] *All have turned away,*
> *they have together become worthless;*
> *there is no one who does good,*
> *not even one."*
> [13] *"Their throats are open graves;*
> *their tongues practice deceit."*
> *"The poison of vipers is on their lips."*
> [14] *"Their mouths are full of cursing and bitterness."*
> [15] *"Their feet are swift to shed blood;*
> [16] *ruin and misery mark their ways,*

> [17] *and the way of peace they do not know."*
>
> [18] *"There is no fear of God before their eyes."*

[19] *Now we know that whatever the law says, it says to those who are under the law, so that every mouth may be silenced and the whole world held accountable to God.* [20] *Therefore no one will be declared righteous in God's sight by the works of the law; rather, through the law we become conscious of our sin.*

The question that opens today's passage opened the previous one. The question is "Do we [Jews] have any advantage?" (3:9). Or, more literally, "Are we [Jews] ahead?" The subtle little problem is that Paul asked almost the same question in 3:1 with a positive answer: "Much in every way!" (3:2). But now he gives a negative answer. So, which is it? Romans 3:9 answers the question and at the same time transforms how we read 3:1–8. Today's passage levels all humans before God, and our passage points a long finger at the human tendency to stereotype others. The Judge of 2:1 represents the person who turned himself into a god-like figure of judgment in chapter one. The stereotyper-of-others is no better than the pagan idolater. Which means he's telling both the Powerful and the Powerless of Romans 14–15 to knock it off because *they are all sinners, all saved by God's grace, all saved by faith, all siblings to one another, and all called to become agents of Christ in this world.*

Everyone and No One

Paul's answer in 3:9 ("Jews and Gentiles alike are all under the power of sin") makes it abundantly clear that possession of the law, or of any of the privileges Israel has as God's covenant people, needs to be put in a better context. Knowing the law does not mean doing the law. Not doing the law makes a person a sinner. Jews, then, are no different than gentiles if they sin. (And they all do.)

All, "Jews and Gentiles," the NIV translates, "are under the power of sin" (3:9) but Paul does not use the term "power" here. He merely says they are all "under sin," and the power of sin—as Romans 6 will show—approximates Paul's meaning. But the NIV offers a more specific translation than what Paul wrote. His words suggest rather that Sin rules over them and sits on its tidy little throne with an accusing finger pointing at every human. Paul turns Sin into an agent with the power to act and control and influence. All are "under Sin," the agent of death.

The stereotyping of gentiles as the world's sinners left that Judge thinking Jewish believers were better than the gentiles because they weren't doing what the gentiles were doing. Which was true almost to a person. But that does not mean they weren't sinners. By the way, Jews knew they were sinners at some level because they yearly celebrated Yom Kippur, the Day of Atonement, at which festival they confessed their sin and were absolved of the year's sins. Paul's intent here is not that kind of concern. His concern is their stereotyping gentiles as idolaters. Their becoming judges. A sin as old as Adam and Eve, Cain and Abel.

Paul has no space for those who think they are not sinners, so he creates a litany of "no one" texts from the Bible that shows everyone has been captured by Agent Sin, and here Paul is exaggerating for effect as the original texts were at times using hyperbole. If you look at the references given in a study Bible, you will discover Paul citing the following: Ecclesiastes 7:20; Psalms 14:1–3; 53:1–3; 5:9; 140:3; 10:7; Isaiah 59:7–8; Proverbs 1:16; Psalm 36:1.

No one is righteous.
No one understands.

No one seeks God.
All turn away from God.
Everyone has become worthless.
No one does good.
Everyone is an open grave of deceit and poison and
cursing and bitterness.
Everyone sheds blood.
No one knows the way of peace.
No one fears God.

If you read those Old Testament verses, you will see that most of them are directed at gentiles, and in this passage he includes his Jewish contemporaries. Stunningly offensive for some. Paul levels the ground to say we all are sinners, gripped by the ugly claws of Agent Sin. No exceptions. Sin here is like the Ring that possessed Gollum in *The Lord of the Rings*.

Including Those with the Privilege of the Law

The concerns turn once again back to the Judge of Romans 2. The law, which Paul just quoted (3:10–18), speaks to those who are "under the law," that is to Israel, to Jews, to the Weak or the Powerless. The impact of the law of God at one level is to unmask humans to reveal their sinfulness (3:19). But there's more to it than that. No one can be justified, or righted, with God (NIV has "declared right" but "declared" is added by translators) by adhering to the law. One of Paul's favorites is "works of the law," which in Paul's letters almost always points at those laws of Moses that Jews practice that at the same time distinguish them from gentile sinners.

Remember where this letter lands: in Rome, looking at both the Powerless and the Powerful, and instructing them to welcome one another because they are siblings in Christ, baptized into Christ, and the Spirit is (supposed to be) at work in them to make them so Christlike they accept anyone accepted by Christ. Stereotypers stereotype.

Stereotypers do not recognize their own sins. The many pastors and churches and priests who have been accused in the last few decades of the deeply wounding sins of abuse, whether sexual or power or emotional or psychological or spiritual or pastoral or financial, have been confronted by their accusers with evidence after evidence and nearly all of them deny, deny, deny. Those are the sorts Paul has his eyes on from Romans 1:18 to 3:20. Yes, what he says is true of all humans, but his deeper concern is to confront the stereotyper for his inconsistency, hypocrisy, and failure to acknowledge, confess, and repent.

In Romans 3–4 there are three basic questions, and our last two passages (3:1–8 and 3:9–20) asked a series of questions that are summarized in one question: Does the one who inherits the law of Moses have an advantage? Now a second question will be about boasting (3:27–31), and the third one will probe a question about Abraham, circumcision, faith, and being right with God (4:1–25). But before we get to that second question, Paul interrupts his intense Q&A in a sentence that packs together major words in his dictionary about redemption in Christ.

Questions for Reflection and Application

1. In what ways does the power of sin impact both Jews and gentiles?

2. How does it change your understanding of Sin to view it as an agent with power?

3. How does God's law work to unmask sinners?

4. What effect does reading the list of Old Testament citations about sin have on you?

5. Do you ever struggle to accept anyone and everyone accepted by Christ? Are you tempted to want to exclude some people from God's welcome?

REDEMPTION WORDS FOR REDEMPTIVE PEACE

Romans 3:21–26

[21] But now apart from the law the righteousness of God has been made known, to which the Law and the Prophets testify. [22] This righteousness is given through faith[fulness] in [of] Jesus Christ to all who believe. There is no difference between Jew and Gentile, [23] for all have sinned and fall short of the glory of God, [24] and all are justified freely by his grace through the redemption that came by Christ Jesus. [25] God presented Christ as a sacrifice of atonement, through the shedding of his blood—to be received by faith. He did this to demonstrate his righteousness, because in his forbearance he had left the sins committed beforehand unpunished—[26] he did it to demonstrate his righteousness at the present time, so as to be just and the one who justifies those who have faith[fulness] in [of] Jesus.

For many readers of Romans, today's passage concludes Paul's case: everyone sins and Christ alone redeems. Yes, everyone's a sinner and redemption is only in Christ, but Romans continues on in chapter four just as it did in chapters two and three with more questions for the audience. Today's passage then is not the conclusion to an argument. Instead, this famous passage interrupts the argument and functions a bit like a sidebar.

Imagine Phoebe in a room with all eyes fixed on her intense reading of all these questions suddenly pausing and, with a pastoral tone, saying, "I've got to clarify something because this is getting intense and long. I'm about to read to you the heart of what the apostle Paul has been teaching for two decades about salvation. Here are Paul's favorite terms tumbling all over one another. Hold on because there's lots to learn." The theoretical nature that makes Romans so famous and influential in the history of Christian thinking is illustrated in today's reading, so read it slowly again.

The major terms of redemption solve some human experience, pain, or wound. Paul's terms for redemption tell personal stories of redemption because these terms fit human experiences. Here are some questions that prompt our thinking about such experiences:

Do you feel not-right with God? Or out of sync and sorts with God?

Do you feel like you cannot do enough to satisfy what you perceive as religious requirements to be considered acceptable in your religious community or small group?

Do you feel enslaved or trapped in some sin or system or social, ethnic, economic, educational category?

Do you feel you have done something that needs to be dealt with, put away, wiped from your conscience?

Do you feel you somehow deserve condemnation for what you have done?

Paul's terms are for you: justification, grace, redemption, atonement, forgiven and declared acceptable and accepted by God.

Redemption Words

God's righteousness (3:21) describes an attribute of God–he is right and does what is right and does it faithfully and always—as well as God's plan for all of creation. He plans to right the ship of creation gone wrong, as it were. He plans to make you and me and all creation right. Righteousness then describes not just an attribute of God but a gift from God to humans. We become right with God through God's grace (see below) that declares us right, makes us right, and empowers to become agents of what is right ("right" can be translated just as accurately with "just").

Being right with God does not occur through the law (3:19–20, 21) but through Jesus Christ, and in 3:22 Paul uses an expression that has generated lots of discussion in the last five decades. Notice these two translations:

> God's righteousness comes "through faith in Jesus Christ" (NIV) and
> God's righteousness comes "through the faithfulness of Jesus Christ" (CEB).

The Greek expression, all must admit, does not specify either. The Greek expression, literally, is *"faith/faithfulness"* (same term) *"of Jesus Christ."* Can we decide one over the other? Consider this. Romans 3:22 finishes with "for all who have faith in him," and because it would be unnecessary to say it again if he had just said "faith in Jesus Christ" (first line, the NIV indented above), of these two options I prefer "through the faithfulness of Jesus Christ." Or perhaps we should just leave it less clear, like the Greek, which literally could be translated "through a Jesus-Christ-faith." Both our need for faith, and Jesus's own faithfulness are true. Jesus was faithful and we are called to have faith in the Jesus who was faithful, and his faithfulness empowers us to be faithful too!

Verse twenty-two ends with a real thud for many: "For there is no difference between Jews and Gentiles." I can hear not a few in the room grumbling "Wha? Yes, there is! Some evening when you finally get to Rome, Mr. Apostle Paul, just take a stroll over to the forum area in Rome. You'll be shocked at the behavior of those gentiles!" To which Paul would say, "Yes, I may be surprised, but it doesn't change my argument," because "all have *sinned*" (3:23). To sin is to violate the law of Moses. And Paul's concept of sin exceeds the view of his entire audience because he affirms sin as a cosmic agent, an agent set loose by Adam and Eve that constrains humans into acts of sin against what God says and what they all know to be right (Romans 5:12–21; 6:1–14). Since all sin, all "fall short of" a life that alone promotes the "glory of God" (3:23).

If all are sinners, then "all" can only be "*justified* by his grace through the redemption that came by Jesus Christ" (3:24). To be justified is to be made right with the God who is rightness in Person. Our experiences of being out of sorts with God, with ourselves, and with others resolve themselves into this wonderful term justification. To be justified then is to be shifted from a ledger called Sinners to a ledger called Saints. The word translated in the NIV with "justified" is *dikaioō*, and that italicized word has the same root as "*righteousness* of God" (*dikaiosynē*) in 3:21. To be justified then means to be made right in accordance with God's own righteousness and God's right-making work.

The work of God in this massive basket of "right" words happen "freely" or "as a gift" of God "by his *grace*." Grace refers to God's own gift-giving to humans. It refers to a gift that a person both knows and feels she does not deserve, and in fact cannot earn. Gift, after all, is gift. A gift given forms a relationship of the Giver with the Receiver, a relationship that prompts not only gratitude but also giving back to God and to others as the proper response to the Gift. There are, according to a recent brilliant study of grace, six possible emphases to this idea of Gift or Grace: (1) it can be superabundant, (2) it can derive from a God who is singularly gracious in all God does, (3) it can emphasize the priority of God being the first to act in the relationship, (4) it can emphasize (as it does in Paul) the Receiver (sinful humans) being unworthy of the Gift, and thus an incongruity between the status of the Giver and the Receiver, (5) it can emphasize the impact on the Receiver in becoming an agent of grace, and (6) it can become a one-way act of Giving that does not draw out a response of reciprocity in the Receiver, though one can question if this is in Paul (see John Barclay, *Paul and the Gift*, 185–186).

What is justification?

Michael Gorman, known at times for long sentences, defines justification as follows: "the establishment of right covenant relations with God, including fidelity to God and love for neighbor, and incorporation into the covenant community of the just/righteous inhabited by the Holy Spirit, the presence of God, by fully identifying with (and thus participating in) the liberating death and resurrection of Jesus" (Gorman, *Romans*, 128).

Paul raided the dictionaries of the ancient world for describing what Jesus accomplished in his life, death, burial, resurrection, and ascension. In this passage alone Paul describes the expansive benefits of the gospel with these terms: God's righteousness, justified freely, redemption, and atonement. Romans 4:25 keeps us on track: his death leads to forgiveness and his resurrection to our justification, or rightness with God. In this passage the word *redemption* describes an enslaved person being set free from sin, death, and cosmic, systemic evil so they can be liberated to live a life free of those menaces. It can be translated "liberation." The human feeling of being trapped in some sinful habit, some systemic category from which there seems to be no release point, or some human propensity that one cannot resist—these experiences are resolved in this wonderful term "redemption." But these slaves to sin are liberated with a price: "by Jesus Christ" and his atoning death "through the shedding of blood." It is God who "presented" Jesus as the liberation price (3:25). In the death and resurrection of Jesus, God revealed something utterly new, and what God reveals establishes a new reality. Paul calls this "new creation" (2 Corinthians 5:17).

God revealed or "presented" Jesus "Christ as a *sacrifice of atonement*" (NIV; 3:25). That translation can be slightly improved to "place of mercy" or the "mercy seat" in the temple, or even the "place of atonement." Notice he says that Jesus becomes the place of mercy and that his blood is sprinkled on that place of mercy. Humans have always established places and shrines and temples for atonement. Those places formed out of the human sensation of guilt and having done something wrong, horrible or less so, and feel they have offended the gods or God. Humans both want and feel the need of atonement. Christ is himself that atonement and resolves our sense of guilt.

Jesus is both the sacrifice and the place where the sacrifice is offered. Which fits with what Paul says in 3:26 when he says God's act of redemption in Christ makes it possible for God to be both *"just" and the "justifier."* What is hidden in the English term "just" at work here is clearer if we use "right" and "right-making." God remains true to being altogether right when God makes us right by moving us from the Sinner ledger to the Saints ledger. God does this through what Jesus did in his earthly life, which is a good reason for us to think of the "faithfulness of Jesus Christ" again (3:22, 26). Verse twenty-six ends, and I translate, with "right and the right-maker of one on the basis of the Jesus-allegiance," that is, the faithfulness of Jesus. Or, possibly, the kind of faithfulness by us that is like the faithfulness of Jesus himself.

One More Time

Paul may not have been what we would call an academic, but he could deal with those who liked to discuss theology. He developed his own vocabulary. At the heart of it is this: all humans sin; God's grace is abundant and profusive in God's love for us; God's Son, Jesus, lived the right life and died a death that benefits us; trusting in Jesus gives us by God's grace all the benefits of salvation.

Paul's clarification is intense, but it cuts off at the knees anyone who thinks following the law of Moses will lead to being right with God. No, to be right with God one must trust in Jesus Christ. From verse twenty-one on Paul clarifies God revealing God's own righteousness and right-making through Jesus Christ.

Paul even here has his eyes on those opponents of his who have been arguing with him ever since he started his mission. They claim the Bible, that God gave the law for all time for all those who want to be in covenant with God. Paul claims Jesus is the fulfillment of that law, that the Spirit empowers people to live as God wants, and that their rightness with God comes through trusting in the Right One, Jesus, not through observance of the law. But what about their advantage? Paul turns to that question again but this time with a new word, boasting. But that's our next passage.

Questions for Reflection and Application

1. What might have been the impact of Paul's "sidebar conversation" in this passage on Phoebe's listeners?

2. Which translation of Jesus-Christ-faith do you favor? "Through faith in Jesus Christ" or "through the faithfulness of Jesus Christ"? Why?

3. Look at the sidebar on justification. Break Gorman's definition down into the various elements to better understand it. What do you think of his definition?

4. How does Barclay's list of emphases about the gift of grace change your understanding of grace?

5. Which of Paul's words about redemption is most impactful to you? Why?

FOR FURTHER READING

John M.G. Barclay, *Paul and the Gift* (Grand Rapids: Wm. B. Eerdmans, 2015).

NO MORE BOASTING IN REDEMPTIVE PEACE

Romans 3:27–31

[27] ***Where, then, is boasting?***

It is excluded.

Because of what law?

The law that requires works?

No, because of the law that requires faith. [28] *For we maintain that a person is justified by faith apart from the works of the law.*

[29] ***Or is God the God of Jews only?***

Is he not the God of Gentiles too?

Yes, of Gentiles too, [30] *since there is only one God, who will justify the circumcised by faith and the uncircumcised through that same faith.*

[31] ***Do we, then, nullify the law by this faith?***

Not at all! Rather, we uphold the law.

Moving from Romans 3:21–26's cascade of terms about God's gracious redemption to the opening question in today's passage—"Where, then, is boasting?"—is a bit like thinking you have been climbing to the mountain top only to realize you've actually circled back to where you began. The question about boasting takes us right back to the Q&A

format of previous passages. In fact, the question echoes what Paul said about the Judge in 2:17 and 2:23: "If you call yourself a Jew . . . and *boast* in God" and "You who *boast* in the law."

We have every reason to think Paul still wants Phoebe to keep her eyes on the Powerless who are stereotyping the Powerful. Reading from Romans aloud to them, she piles one question on top of another (which I have put in bold font again). The intensity can't be ignored.

Boasting Re-Considered

In the house churches of Rome are some people who claimed privilege. First, the Powerful, or Strong, may have been more connected to Roman upper-class people of privilege, and in that world, one was expected to boast about one's status. It was not so much bragging as it was social self-affirmation of what one deserved. People with potential acquired public honor through military victories, through distribution of their wealth, through appearance, through associations and networks (called patronage), and through oratorical ability. Not to affirm one's status, or boast about one's status, was to degrade oneself. And self-humiliating jokes were not the way of the Romans. So, some Strong knew the way of boasting as something virtuous. Second, the Powerless claimed privilege because of their divine election, as the second chapter of Romans makes clear. These are the contexts for Paul's sudden shift to the theme of boasting. Remember, for both the Strong and the Weak, *boasting was virtuous* and not a sin.

Boasting Re-Imagined

Paul had some choice words for this all-too-common "virtue" running from home to home in the house churches of Rome. Boasting, he says, "is excluded" or "is shut out" (3:27). *Don't even let it in the room*, Phoebe must be muttering as she read this letter. All boasting turns one group into superior and another into inferior, an "in crowd" and an "out crowd." C.S. Lewis once described the inside circle in social groups as the "inner ring" (*The Weight of Glory*, 141–157). Again, both the Powerful and the Powerless boasted they were the inner ring.

A rough contemporary of Lewis was George Orwell, whose own experience at a status-driven school reveals that the way of Rome finds a way in all societies. Here he describes the social reality at his grammar school:

> That was the pattern of school life–a continuous triumph of the strong over the weak. Virtue consisted in winning: it consisted in being bigger, stronger, handsomer, richer, more popular, more elegant, more unscrupulous than other people–in dominating them, bullying them, making them suffer pain, making them look foolish, getting the better of them in every way. Life was hierarchical and whatever happened was right. There were the strong, who deserved to win and always did win, and there were the weak, who deserved to lose and always lose, everlastingly.

Maybe the saddest line in his description of school days is "I did not possess any of these qualities" (Orwell, *In Front of Your Nose*, 359). He wrote that many years later with a bitter twist and a hot pen. I wonder how many of us experienced a kind of "losing" in our grade school days that either marked us for life or shaped us in ways that required healing. The all-too-human chase for status nearly always requires someone else being degraded.

In his torrent of fast-moving words Paul contends boasting of one's status, honor, privilege, or accomplishment is shut out of the room because redemption for the Weak is not based on their observance ("works") of the law of Moses but on the basis of faith. Which one more time levels everyone, Jew and gentile, Powerless and Powerful. Paul's question, "Is God the God of the Jews only?" is a question with "No" for an answer, and the answer is another level-er. God is the God of *both Jews and gentiles*. If one boasts in one's status for observing the law of Moses, one degrades the gentile believer who doesn't observe the law. If one gives status to the one who believes in Christ, one upgrades everyone. That kind of upgrade can be described as redemptive peace at work among the believers.

Paul ends with a tantalizing line. Make that yet another question, this one based on the necessity of faith and not observance of the law: "Do we, then, nullify the law?" Nope, and here comes the surprise: "we uphold the law" or cause it to stand up straight! (3:31).

That had to surprise some of those listening to Phoebe read the letter. What Paul means by straightening up the law will become clear in Romans 4.

Questions for Reflection and Application

1. How did status work in the Roman world?

2. What was the understanding of boasting in Roman culture? How does this context help you better understand Paul's words on boasting?

3. How does God work as a level-er of status?

4. Can you recall experiences of feeling less-than as Orwell describes? What comes to mind?

5. How have other people degraded you in their quest for status? How have you degraded others in your own efforts to move up a hierarchy?

FOR FURTHER READING

C.S. Lewis, *The Weight of Glory, and Other Addresses* (SanFrancisco: HarperSanFrancisco, 2001).

George Orwell, *The Collected Essays, Journalism & Letters*. Volume 4: *In Front of Your Nose, 1946–1950* (ed. Sonia Orwell, Ian Angus; Boston: Nonpareil Books/David R. Godine, 2000). The words come from his famous essay "Such, Such Were the Joys," pp. 330–369, an essay originally published in 1947, and found in many anthologies.

ABRAHAM'S GOD AND REDEMPTIVE PEACE

Romans 4:1–25

[1] ***What then shall we say that Abraham, our forefather according to the flesh, discovered in this matter?***

[2] *If, in fact, Abraham was justified by works, he had something to boast about—but not before God.*

[3] ***What does Scripture say?***

"Abraham believed God, and it was credited to him as righteousness."

[4] *Now to the one who works, wages are not credited as a gift but as an obligation.* [5] *However, to the one who does not work but trusts God who justifies the ungodly, their faith is credited as righteousness.* [6] *David says the same thing when he speaks of the blessedness of the one to whom God credits righteousness apart from works:*

[7] *"Blessed are those*
whose transgressions are forgiven,
whose sins are covered.
[8] *Blessed is the one*
whose sin the Lord will never count against them."

[9] ***Is this blessedness only for the circumcised, or also for the uncircumcised?***

We have been saying that Abraham's faith was credited to him as righteousness.

[10] **Under what circumstances was it credited?**

Was it after he was circumcised, or before?

It was not after, but before! [11] *And he received circumcision as a sign, a seal of the righteousness that he had by faith while he was still uncircumcised. So then, he is the father of all who believe but have not been circumcised, in order that righteousness might be credited to them.* [12] *And he is then also the father of the circumcised who not only are circumcised but who also follow in the footsteps of the faith that our father Abraham had before he was circumcised.*

[13] *It was not through the law that Abraham and his offspring received the promise that he would be heir of the world, but through the righteousness that comes by faith.* [14] *For if those who depend on the law are heirs, faith means nothing and the promise is worthless,* [15] *because the law brings wrath. And where there is no law there is no transgression.*

[16] *Therefore, the promise comes by faith, so that it may be by grace and may be guaranteed to all Abraham's offspring—not only to those who are of the law but also to those who have the faith of Abraham. He is the father of us all.* [17] *As it is written: "I have made you a father of many nations." He is our father in the sight of God, in whom he believed—the God who gives life to the dead and calls into being things that were not.*

[18] *Against all hope, Abraham in hope believed and so became the father of many nations, just as it had been said to him, "So shall your offspring be."* [19] *Without weakening in his faith, he faced the fact that his body was as good as dead—since he was about a hundred years old—and that Sarah's womb was also dead.* [20] *Yet he did not waver through unbelief regarding the promise of God, but was strengthened in his faith and gave glory to God,* [21] *being fully persuaded that God had power to do what he had promised.* [22] *This is why "it was credited to him as righteousness."* [23] *The words "it*

was credited to him" were written not for him alone, [24] *but also for us, to whom God will credit righteousness—for us who believe in him who raised Jesus our Lord from the dead.* [25] *He was delivered over to death for our sins and was raised to life for our justification.*

There is tension among believers in Rome, and the apostle writes this letter to them because he believes redemption in Christ creates a new kind of peace that can be achieved between people with different histories and habits. Romans 1:18–4:25 puts quill to papyrus what Paul has learned in responding to those who disagree with his approach to gospel preaching and what is expected of gentile converts to Jesus. His basic argument is that all believers are sinners saved by faith in Jesus, and therefore they are one in Christ. Redemption in Christ empowers peace between siblings in Christ. Unity in Christ looks good on paper, but so too did the Roman empire until you happened to live in Gaul or Brittania. Rome's vaunted *Pax Romana* easily became bloody warfare and domination. War reveals what happens between humans when they become the powers of the state.

Because humans inevitably create conflicts, Paul searched every argument he could find for unity between siblings in Christ. In Romans 4 he forms his final argument before he turns to the solution in chapters five through eight. Paul learned early on that he could appeal to the hero of heroes. Abraham illustrated for Paul his entire case for redemptive peace between the Powerful and the Powerless. The story of Israel in many ways begins with God making covenant with Abraham (Genesis 15; 17). God's promises to Abraham tilled fertile turf for Paul. Paul turns yet again to questions he gets to ask and to answer. Each of these questions also explores the question Paul asked at 3:1 about the advantage "in being a Jew."

Questions

Paul asks essentially five questions,[1] which I have put in bold above, and I slightly adjusted the formatting. After asking each question, Phoebe gave the listeners a moment to consider how they would answer the question. Apart from brand new followers of Jesus, the audience all knew the story of Abraham. From the story of Abraham, Paul is able to demonstrate that Abraham's being made right with God was *before* his circumcision. Therefore, before any "works" had been done. And *if that is true*—and everyone has to agree that it is—then being part of Abraham's family is based on faith, not on circumcision. Notice again how important this single command given to Abraham becomes in Paul's argument. If salvation is by faith, not by works, then a completely different basis forms for unity in the faith. There is no reason for the Weak or the Strong to be unwelcoming of one another at the table if that "another" trusts in Christ. Here are Paul's questions in this passage:

> What then shall we say that Abraham, our forefather according to the flesh, discovered in this matter? (4:1)
>
> What does Scripture say? (4:3)
>
> Is this blessedness only for the circumcised, or also for the uncircumcised? (4:9)
>
> Under what circumstances was it credited? (4:10)
>
> Was it after he was circumcised, or before? (4:10)

Those listening to this letter being read must have been relieved when Paul stopped asking questions after that fifth question. He will only return to this level of Q&A in Romans 9–11.

Questions are asked to get answers. Paul's answers probe nothing less than the theory of redemption.

Answers

Paul answers his own questions just in case the Romans misfire when they provide their own answers. Paul goes "total Bible" on them to answer the questions. Michael Gorman says Paul sees Abraham as both "proof" and "paradigm." What happened to Abraham both *proves* that justification occurs by faith without works and shows that he is the *paradigm* of true faith—trusting in the God who promises (Gorman, *Romans,* 131). "The story about Abraham shows that . . ."

Our Boasting Does Not Work with God

Abraham would have had *something to boast about* if he could have been made right on the basis of works, and the work in mind is either circumcision (Genesis 17) or the act of nearly sacrificing Isaac in Genesis 22. Such boasting would have given him status among humans *"but not before God"* (Romans 4:2). God is the One who matters.

Our Choice Is Either the Faith or the Works System

The second question in 4:3 is answered by quoting Genesis 15:6, one of Paul's favorite verses. Paul pulled this verse out of his memory in every conversation he had with those who questioned his gentile mission. Abraham was made right with God *because he "believed God"* (Romans 4:3). Following his citation of scriptural support, Paul explains what he means (4:4–8). His explanation is simple: a system of "works" assumes an "obligation" the employer has in paying the "wages" the worker earns (4:4). In which case the "wage" is earned; it is not a "gift." But Abraham was made right by God's gift, and God "justifies the ungodly" on the basis of "faith" (4:5). The faith system meshes with the gift system; the works system with the obligation system. The faith system derives from the God system; the works system derives from the human system.

God system	Human system
Gift system	Obligation system
Faith system	Law/works system

Our True Blessedness Means Being Right with God

Paul begins by appealing to Genesis 15 about Abraham, and now turns to David and Psalm 32:1–2, a psalm that delights in God's gracious forgiveness, the importance of transparent confession before God (32:3–5), and the necessity of trusting in God (32:10). As with Abraham so with David: one is made right with God on the basis of trusting God, of faith in the God of goodness and love.

The third question (**Is this blessedness only for the circumcised, or also for the uncircumcised?**) opens up with the word "blessedness" that David gloried in (4:9). The term "blessedness" quickly shifts into the term "righteousness" (4:10). The question is whether that blessing was only for the circumcised, and Paul's answer, given in 4:9, is that the blessing of God making Abraham right came to Abraham on the basis of "faith."

Our Being Made Right with God Occurs before Works

Paul's third question (above) was perhaps not quite clear enough. So he asks a fourth from a different angle: **Was it** [God making Abraham right with God] ***after*** **he was circumcised, or *before*?** This question appeals to Bible Story Basics 101, but the answer plunges into the depths of God's truth. The order of two events matter: (1) God's promise, Abraham's trust, and God's making him righteous (Genesis 15) and (2) God's requiring circumcision (Genesis 17). In which chapter was he considered right with God? Answer: Genesis 15. Question: Which was before or after Genesis 17? Answer: Before. *Therefore,* God making him right happens (1) on the basis of faith and (2) independent of the work of circumcision. *Therefore,* no one can require circumcision, or any other work connected to the later law from Moses, *in order to be made right by God with God.*

He clarifies this a little more. Circumcision is a "sign" or a "seal" that points back to "faith kind of righteousness" (my translation). Here Paul becomes repetitive. Repetition is the mother of all learning. This means Abraham is the "father" of the faith system and the uncircumcised who have faith, and he's the father of the circumcised who have faith in Christ (4:11–12).

Our God's Promise Precedes God's Requirements

For Paul the tension between the Weak and the Strong has a deep biblical answer, and Paul knows his Bible! Not only was Abraham justified by faith, and not only was he made right before he was circumcised, but *the divine promise* was given to him in that faith-righteousness event of Genesis 15.

Again, before the rite of circumcision. That promise forms the foundation for *everything* in Paul's mission to the gentiles. And that promise provides a solution for the problems in Rome. The promise is "that he would be the heir of the world" (4:13) and to "all Abraham's offspring" (4:16) and to "many nations" (4:17, 18). Paul anchors three deep arguments in the story of Abraham:

> righteousness comes by faith not works;
> righteousness comes before circumcision;
> and righteousness comes to gentiles by faith as well.

The faith system for righteousness means the law system is not designed to make people righteous (4:14–15). Paul will develop this even more in Romans 7, and we can wait till then to put that theme together.

Our Faith Is like Abraham's Faith

Faith for Abraham unleashed life *because Abraham had a kind of hope that trusted God* to do something that seemed impossible. This is what I call the "magic" of faith. Abraham and Sarah were not of the age to have children, but God gave them children because God promised they would have children, and Abraham believed that God's word was as good as done. "Against all hope," Paul says, the old man "in hope believed" (4:18), and "faced the fact that his body was as good as dead" (4:19), and "he did not waver through unbelief" and "was strengthened in his faith and gave glory to God" (4:20), and was "fully persuaded that God had power to do what he had promised" (4:21). So God, knowing the faith of Abraham, "credited [it] to him as righteousness" (4:22).

Trust in the God of grace shifted Abraham from the ledger of sin to the ledger of being right with God (4:23–24). Through Christ and faith in Christ we, too, find both forgiveness and being made right (4:25). Not by works of the law, not by circumcision, but by faith. All salvation is salvation through faith.

All the arguments the Powerless offer for gentiles needing to observe the law of Moses have now been put to the test by Paul. He has searched the Scriptures through the covenant God made with Abraham, and he finds the arguments of the Weak deeply mistaken. The tensions in Rome result from a failure to understand what God promised Abraham.

Therefore, welcome one another. Eat with one another as siblings in Christ. You are one in Christ because you are one in the faith that makes one right with God. For now, the argumentativeness of Paul's letter takes a nap. His most important words—God's love, Adam and Christ, baptism, Agent Sin, Agent Life, the law, the Ego, Spirit and Flesh, Suffering, and Victory—form into a network of words about redemptive peace. These words matter, and they matter so much they connect in the network in a way that redefines each one. Before Paul, none of these words meant what they mean for Paul.

Here's a word cloud:[2]

Questions for Reflection and Application

1. How does Paul use the story of Abraham to teach about church unity in the face of tension?

2. How does Paul illustrate that faith is based on faith, not works?

3. What is the difference between a wage system and a gift system?

4. How is Abraham able to be the "father" of both the faithful circumcised and the faithful uncircumcised?

5. With a deeper understanding of oneness in faith, how can you show better welcome to your siblings in Christ?

GOD'S LOVE AND REDEMPTIVE PEACE

Romans 5:1–11

[1] Therefore, since we have been justified through faith, we have peace with God through our Lord Jesus Christ, [2] through whom we have gained access by faith into this grace in which we now stand. And we boast in the hope of the glory of God. [3] Not only so, but we also glory in our sufferings, because we know that suffering produces perseverance; [4] perseverance, character; and character, hope. [5] And hope does not put us to shame, because God's love has been poured out into our hearts through the Holy Spirit, who has been given to us.

[6] You see, at just the right time, when we were still powerless, Christ died for the ungodly. [7] Very rarely will anyone die for a righteous person, though for a good person someone might possibly dare to die. [8] But God demonstrates his own love for us in this: While we were still sinners, Christ died for us.

[9] Since we have now been justified by his blood, how much more shall we be saved from God's wrath through him! [10] For if, while we were God's enemies, we were reconciled to him through the death of his Son, how much more, having been reconciled, shall we be saved through his life! [11] Not only is this so, but we also boast in God through our Lord Jesus Christ, through whom we have now received reconciliation.

When you turn in your Bible from Romans 4 to Romans 5 you will notice a massive shift in tone, in style, and in direction. The tone is much warmer, the style shifts from interrogation through Q&A to straightforward explanation, and the direction is how to live as a follower of Jesus with real-life solutions and experiences and emotions. Paul's real-life solutions for Christian living form into a network of words. So I repeat the words that ended the previous chapter. Paul's most important words—like love, Adam and Christ, baptism, Agent Sin, Agent Life, the law, the Ego, Spirit and Flesh, Suffering, and Victory—form into a network of words about redemptive peace. These words matter, and they matter so much they connect in the network in a way that redefines each one. Before Paul, none of these words meant what they mean for Paul.

What they mean for Paul, too, points directly at the problems in Rome between believers: the Powerful and the Powerless. Think of the Three C's of a church culture, its organization, and its leadership. There is *Coercion*, a top-down, authoritative leader approach. Coercive leadership will eventually lead to conflict that provokes someone or someones to form into *Competition* with the leader. Good leaders reject coercion and have the social skills to promote *Cooperation*, which prevents Competition from appearing. The house churches in Rome are in a Competitive phase, and Paul pleads for Cooperation. Paul's network of words wants to snag Coercion and Competition and overcome them with Cooperation.

One little term gets ignored, and I didn't mention it above. Paul shifts from "you" language in Romans 2–4 to "we" language. In today's passage alone we have we, us, and ours used twenty-three times in the NIV. He has turned from pointing *at* problem people or speaking *to* them to including himself in a mutual reality *with* them. Paul's language becomes a pastoral signal that's he's done (for four chapters) with the interrogation so he can provide for them the solution to the problems they are facing in Rome.

A theology of the Christian life begins with God's unconditioned love, and God's love does at least four things.

God's Love for Us Creates Peace with God

When I was a child our church sang classic hymns, and there were enough good singers who knew how to sing parts that we could at times really roll (but not rock or Rick). One of my favorites was when the good singers harmonized and echoed one another, and then with some songs we (Baptists, so we were careful) swayed with our bodies to words like those in this song:[1]

> It is well (it is well)
> With my soul (with my soul)
> It is well, it is well with my soul.

The song began where Romans 5 begins, and the lyrics probably came from that very verse, beginning with "When peace like a river attendeth my way." If you grew up with this hymn, know that we are now waiting for you to find it on YouTube, listen to it a couple times, and then return to this spot in the book.

You back yet? Let's move on.

Soul peace is an internal contentment in God's love, in God's redemption in Jesus Christ, in God's Spirit prompting that love in our heart, and in a contentment that empowers us to walk forward knowing God is with us and behind us and before us. Those who have peace with God become agents of peace with others. Which means the peace here cannot be reduced to soul-peace because true peace includes peace with others, justice, safety, and health. To be sure, peace with God forms the heart of peace.

Because God has made us right with himself through Christ by faith (or perhaps by the faithfulness of Jesus Christ himself), we have this peace—knowing that "we have gained access by faith into this grace [of righteousness]" (5:2). One cannot sum up what God has done for us with one term, so Paul uses a number here because each adds to the other: justify, peace, access, grace, hope, and glory of God (not our own status). We are to remember that God in Christ justifies, and we participate in that right-making through trust and allegiance. Because God loves us, God justifies; because God justifies, we have peace with God; because we have peace with God, we have peace with one another.

God's Love for Us Permeates Our Hearts

Article I: God's love "has been poured out into our hearts through the Holy Spirit" whom God has given to us (5:5). This set of words describes a permeating, emotional reality deriving from the divine energy at work in the experience of peace in 5:1. Namely, that any "suffering" for Christ that comes our way can be captured—paradoxically—in the word "glory" because in that suffering, we come to know the love of God. Not that Paul likes or minimizes suffering, but he has learned in his own suffering that it can impact us in a good way. It promotes spiritual formation in perseverance, character, and hope (5:4).

Article II: God is love. God made us in his image, and part of that image is our capacity to love God and others and our capacity to experience God's love and the love of others.

To know we are loved by others produces peace in us, but to know we are loved by God produces the deepest peace in the depth of our innermost being.

God's Love Ignores Our Social Status and Forgives Our Sins

Fleming Rutledge, in a sermon at Duke University Chapel, once said, "The one great mistake we could make today is to think of ourselves in the wrong category" (Rutledge, "The Enemy Lines Are Hard to Find," 346). We are not, she observes, the righteous but the sinners. God's love coordinates with our being "powerless" and "ungodly" and "sinners" and "enemies" (5:6–11; recall the "but now" in 3:21). One feels like Paul is using a thesaurus to find words about the benefits of the gospel and the condition of humans who experience the benefits of salvation. Four terms here reveal that God disregards our status in this world, which will have taken a bite out of the ego of anyone stereotyping others or appealing to privilege. God doesn't care if we are the *Powerless*. He loves us and directs his Son's demonstration of cross-love right at all of us.

In fact, God's love becomes the death of Christ for us. His death not only demonstrates God's love and the kind of love God has, and these are both true, but his death embodies God who is love.

His second term is found in "Christ died for the *ungodly*" (5:6). The NIV's "ungodly" is a traditional translation but the term (*asebēs*) in the Roman world was used for those whose public religious practices were socially disrespectable. It was used for Romans and Greeks who did not attend public ceremonies, traditional celebrations, and religious events. So, "ungodly" works as long as we keep in mind that the "god" in "ungodly" was not just the one true God but also the gods of their world. Thus, this terms coordinates with the powerless term. Jesus died for those who didn't give a flip about religion or custom or tradition and who were hence powerless in the Roman world.

A third term is *sinners*. Sinners are those who "miss the mark" when shooting an arrow. But it can mean to miss, to fail, to lack, to fall short, to offend, and even to be mistaken. In a Jewish worldview a sinner ignores or chooses to violate a law of God or a traditional rule derived from interpreting the law of God. A "righteous person" or a "good person" (5:7–8) does the will of God consistently.

The final term is *enemies* (5:10), humans hostile toward God and God's will, who rebel against God, who fight God, and who violate God's will intentionally and flagrantly and even publicly. We can imagine those who thumb their nose to God.

It does not matter if we are powerless and publicly irreligious, nor does it matter if we are sinners and hostile toward God—God loves us, God sent his Son for us, and his Son has died for us so we can turn to God in faith and be transformed by the Spirit into agents of love for all humans, especially everyone in the family of Jesus. God's love for us makes no sense, and no one has said this more forcefully than Peter Groves:

> Love makes no sense. It is unsettling, undermining, deconstructive. It turns our world upside down, challenges all our preconceptions, invites us to reconsider the whole of our lives now that love has arrived on the scene. The absurdity of Christianity is not just that the love that makes no sense is the truth that we find in Jesus of Nazareth. The real absurdity of Christianity

> is the claim that that love is what we are talking about when we are talking about God himself. God is love, and love makes no sense (Strawbridge, Mercer, Groves, *Love Makes No Sense*, 10–11).

When Jesus taught his disciples to love their enemies (Matthew 5:43–48), he was on a mission from the Father to demonstrate, teach, and embody that love in a death that redefined love—a love that, yes, seems to make no sense *until you know it does.*

God's Love for Us Generates Eternal Life

Everyone dies. Those who were following Jesus also knew that any of them could disappear that day into the dungeons of persecution and suffering and death. Following death, each person faces God. Paul turns now to how God's unconditioned love shapes how to face the future. Because God made us right through the death and resurrection of Jesus (4:25), we are not only saved *now* but we will be saved *in the future* "from God's wrath" (5:9). In the Bible the anger of God comes to expression against those who rebel against God knowingly. It's a kind of inner being repulsion by God toward what is so un-God-like or what is non-God.

> If we are justified, we will be saved from that wrath.
>
> If we are reconciled, we will be "saved through his life" (5:10).
>
> If all this is true, we now no longer boast about ourselves but we boast in Christ alone (5:11).

One sentence summary: the Christian life begins in the love of God and knows by experience that God loves us and that God's love works in us to transform all of life, including our bodies.

Questions for Reflection and Application

1. How does Paul's shift from "you" to "we" signal a change in his approach in chapter 5?

2. What do you think Paul's personal sufferings taught him about God's love?

3. How does God's love work to generate emotions like love, hope, and peace in God's people?

4. When have you seen Coercion, Competition, and Cooperation in church cultures? How did you feel in the presence of each?

5. Of the four things God's love does for us, which feels most impactful to you? Why?

FOR FURTHER READING

Fleming Rutledge, "The Enemy Lines Are Hard to Find," in William H. Willimon, ed., *Sermons from Duke Chapel: Voices from "A Great Towering Church"* (Durham: Duke University Press, 2005), 342–347.

Jennifer Strawbridge, Jarred Mercer, Peter Groves, *Love Makes No Sense: An Invitation to Christian Theology* (London: SCM, 2019).

ADAM, CHRIST, AND REDEMPTIVE PEACE

Romans 5:12–21

[12] Therefore, just as sin entered the world through one man, and death through sin, and in this way death came to all people, because all sinned—

[13] To be sure, sin was in the world before the law was given, but sin is not charged against anyone's account where there is no law. [14] Nevertheless, death reigned from the time of Adam to the time of Moses, even over those who did not sin by breaking a command, as did Adam, who is a pattern of the one to come.

[15] But the gift is not like the trespass. For if the many died by the trespass of the one man, how much more did God's grace and the gift that came by the grace of the one man, Jesus Christ, overflow to the many! [16] Nor can the gift of God be compared with the result of one man's sin: The judgment followed one sin and brought condemnation, but the gift followed many trespasses and brought justification. [17] For if, by the trespass of the one man, death reigned through that one man, how much more will those who receive God's abundant provision of grace and of the gift of righteousness reign in life through the one man, Jesus Christ!

[18] Consequently, just as one trespass resulted in condemnation for all people, so also one righteous act resulted in justification and

life for all people. [19] *For just as through the disobedience of the one man the many were made sinners, so also through the obedience of the one man the many will be made righteous.*

[20] *The law was brought in so that the trespass might increase. But where sin increased, grace increased all the more,* [21] *so that, just as sin reigned in death, so also grace might reign through righteousness to bring eternal life through Jesus Christ our Lord.*

The first Christian life word is that God *loves* us, and we learn in today's passage that God loves *all the Adams and Eves* in this world. In spite of what Adam and Eve did in the Garden of Eden, God not only loves us but God draws us into his circle of love so we can be healed of the impact of Adam and Eve on us. Yes, I add Eve even if Paul didn't! God's love for us is so intense, God sent his Son, Christ, to undo the damage of Eden and to set in motion a new reality in Christ.

It's at least fun at times to play the "There are two kinds of people" game. Two kinds of writers—those who outline a whole book before they write an actual word, and those who figure out what to write by writing. Two kinds of parents—helicopter parents and "let 'em learn on their own" parents. Two kinds of police—those who serve the community and those who assert their authority. Two kinds of bosses—those who boss everyone around and those who build relationships of trust. Two kinds of cultures—tov and toxic. (Tov is a Hebrew word meaning goodness in all its dimensions.)

For Paul, there are two kinds of people: those in line behind Adam and those in line behind Christ. He's not exaggerating for the sake of emphasis. He's not playing a "there are two kinds of people" game. He's truth-telling. Redemption transfers a person from the Adam line to the Christ line. What one did, the other undid. And not only did he undo the Adam line, but his undoing far transcended the doing. If

I give you something and you give me something back, we call that reciprocity. If I give you something and you give me something more valuable back, we call that generosity. If I steal something from you and you give me something I wanted so deeply that I didn't even know what it was or that I wanted it, we call that God's expansive grace. Which is what Paul explains in today's passage. The best way I know how to explain this passage is to read through it to see what we discover about the Adam line and then another reading to discover the Christ line. Two words that explain the Christian life for Paul: Adam and Christ. Two words that also explain the problems in the Roman churches: believers living like Adam and believers needing to live like Christ.

Adam Line

There is a progression of ideas in what Paul says about Adam. He adds things as he goes along. What is true of Adam becomes true of All in Paul's sketch of Two Kinds of People. What Adam did, all did; what resulted for Adam, resulted for all. Adam's sin's impact on other can be explained as a systemic distortion of the world.

If you are reading the NIV, you will see that 5:12 is an incomplete sentence. The "just as" in 5:12 is not completed in until 5:18. Just how Phoebe hung her audiences in the balance that long is something worth thinking about.

Adam

God created Adam, and Paul here does a typical Jewish thing by ignoring Eve.

Adam, the one man, "sinned" (*hamartia*; 5:12), "trespassed" (*paraptōma*; 5:15) and was in "disobedience" (*parakoē*; 5:19).

Adam's sin leads to divine "judgment" and "condemnation" (5:16).
Adam's sin led to "death" for Adam.
Sinning promoted Sin as an agent that is at work this world.

All

Adam's sinning somehow passes on to "all" and all sin (5:12).
There is "sin" already "in the world" before there was "law."
God reveals his law through Moses to the people of Israel.
That revelation exacerbated sinning into a deeper level of SIN (5:13–14, 20).
All humans through sin are judged and condemned (5:18).
All humans die because, like Adam, all humans sin (5:12, 15).
Death reigns (5:17).
Death is the destiny of the Adam line.

Christ Line

As said above, Christ is the Great Undoing (and more) of what Adam did and of the results Adam experienced due to his sin. But Christ also undoes all that all humans have done and all that all humans experienced because of that sin. All this occurs through Christ. Christ's act of obedience can be seen as a systemic realignment of the world with God. As Thomas L. Hoyt, Jr., says it, Adam's sin led to "an existence that is blighted by a defective relationship with God" (Hoyt, "Romans," 257). Christ reverses the curse and creates a whole new reality.

Christ

Christ is God's "gift" (*charisma*; 5:15) and "grace" (*charis*; 5:15, 20).
Christ brings "justification" (5:16, 18), "life" and "righteousness" (5:17, 18, 19).
Christ performs "one righteous act" (5:18) = his death and resurrection (4:25).
Christ's grace-gift overwhelms and overcomes the "trespass" (5:20).
Christ's act of grace promotes life and Life becomes an agent in this world.

All/Many

God's grace-gift "overflowed" to "many" (5:15).
The "many trespasses" of all results in "justification" (5:16), "life" and "righteousness" (5:17, 19).
The All/Many "receive" the gift (5:17).
For "all people" (5:18).
Life eternal reigns (5:17, 21).

This all begs for some explanations. The secret sauce of Paul's theology is who Christ is and what Christ accomplishes. In the plan of history Adam's "contribution" is sin and death, but God enters that history in the flesh in Jesus to remedy sin, to rectify humans, and to reestablish humans into a life that leads to eternal life. Jesus undoes the damage done by Adam. As such, Jesus is the Second Adam establishing new creation. But his Undoing far transcends the damage done. Death is not only defeated, but new life replaces it.

Paul points both at Adam (and Eve) and at humans. Michael Gorman warns us that this passage does not say we inherit Adam's sin through sexual intercourse but that we affirm and reaffirm Adam's sin in our sinning (Gorman, *Romans,* 158–159). The Jewish world before Paul over and over saw Adam and Eve as types of sinners but they did not hold all humans guilty before God because Adam and Eve sinned (Venema and McKnight, *Adam and the Genome,* 111–169).

God's love undoes death and establishes new life in and through Christ. Those who participate in Christ—who trust in him, who are faithful to him, who obey him, who follow him—will enter into life now and in eternity. Those who trust in him do so because they are empowered by God's grace in the Spirit of God and, in being united with Christ through that faith, are empowered to become obedient followers of Jesus (Romans 12:1–2).

A Christian Approach to "All"

Those who are in the Christ line often develop feelings, thoughts, attitudes, dispositions, and actions toward those in the Adam line that conform to how Christ felt about the Adam line. Christ is love, the compass of compassion, the ruler of right living, the friend of the friendless, the inviter of the uninvited . . . we could go on. We are called to follow Christ and to offer him to the Adam-ites of our world. In the Christ line any and every human can experience freedom from Adam's sin, from sin, and from Sin increased by law. One can experience an absence of a fear of death. More importantly, one can discover a life of love, righteousness, peace, and goodness.

God's grace-gift is magnificent enough to cover *all* sins, to encompass *all* humans, and to congratulate *all* into this presence. Notice how often *all* is used in today's passage. I suggest underlining each one to impress upon the mind that what Adam did to all, Christ undid for all. But the people in "all" in Romans 5 experience the graces of what Christ accomplishes only through trust in God's wonderful act in Jesus Christ. Our posture then toward the Adam line is the posture of God, which is the relentless offer of grace. Justification, or God's making us right, is a "death-defeating, life-giving, transformative reality" (Gorman, *Romans*, 162, all italics in original).

If the Second Adam overcomes the damage of the First Adam, all who believe experience the same grace, receive the same gift of being right, and that means all in Christ are equally graced. Therefore, the Romans should cease their divisions at the table because All are invited.

Questions for Reflection and Application

1. What are the differences between the Adam line and the Christ line?

2. How does sin come to All people through Adam?

3. How does Christ provide freedom from sin and Sin?

4. Go through the passage again and underline the uses of "all." What do you notice?

5. How does the understanding that All are invited impact your understanding of church unity?

FOR FURTHER READING

Dennis R. Venema, Scot McKnight, *Adam and the Genome: Reading Scripture after Genetic Science* (Grand Rapids: Brazos, 2017).

BAPTISM AND REDEMPTIVE PEACE

Romans 6:1–14

[1] ***What shall we say, then?***

Shall we go on sinning so that grace may increase?

[2] *By no means!*

We are those who have died to sin; ***how can we live in it any longer?***

[3] ***Or don't you know that all of us who were baptized into Christ Jesus were baptized into his death?***

[4] *We were therefore buried with him through baptism into death in order that, just as Christ was raised from the dead through the glory of the Father, we too may live a new life.*

[5] *For if we have been united with him in a death like his, we will certainly also be united with him in a resurrection like his.* [6] *For we know that our old self was crucified with him so that the body ruled by sin might be done away with, that we should no longer be slaves to sin—*[7] *because anyone who has died has been set free from sin.*

[8] *Now if we died with Christ, we believe that we will also live with him.* [9] *For we know that since Christ was raised from the dead, he cannot die again; death no longer has mastery over him.*

[10] The death he died, he died to sin once for all; but the life he lives, he lives to God.

[11] In the same way, count yourselves dead to sin but alive to God in Christ Jesus. [12] Therefore do not let sin reign in your mortal body so that you obey its evil desires. [13] Do not offer any part of yourself to sin as an instrument of wickedness, but rather offer yourselves to God as those who have been brought from death to life; and offer every part of yourself to him as an instrument of righteousness. [14] For sin shall no longer be your master, because you are not under the law, but under grace.

Several Christian life words begin to clarify how God's transforming work occurs, including God's relentless love and grace for us in spite of our sinfulness. And God's love for us in Christ. That love defeats death and launches an entirely new creation for all those in Christ. This new life empowers both the Powerful and the Powerless to leave the line of Adam and walk in the line of Christ.

If Christ undid all Adam did, and if sin magnifies the saving work of God, then why not just sin. After all, it glorifies God?! If lots of sin produces a lot more grace, why not jump all over sin and magnify grace?! This sounds like the Powerful, among whom were plenty of gentile believers with a past. Paul's solution to a cavalier attitude toward sins may surprise. His solution introduces a big Christian life word for Paul. *Baptism*. At least it surprises some. If you are in a more traditional church, you may not be surprised, but if you are in a Baptist or Baptist-like group, you may be surprised. Among such groups, and nearly all non-denominational churches are Baptist-like, baptism is understood as *symbolic* of redemption, but the act *in itself* does not do anything redemptive. Christ accomplished redemption, and our only act is to believe in Christ. That's the major act for the human. Baptism then symbolizes that action.

Paul was not a Baptist, at least like that. Baptism *does* something to a person.

Baptism Does

In the New Testament the act of baptism does something, and what it does is connected to redemption in ways that can challenge the simplistic symbolic view. Baptism in the earliest Christian teaching, and some of that is represented in today's passage, first, leads to union with Christ. We are baptized "in the name of Jesus Christ" (Acts 2:38; Matthew 28:19) and in baptism we are joined to his death and resurrection (Romans 6:3–4). Second, baptism leads to the reception of the Spirit and church's reception of us. Acts 2:38 says this explicitly: "Repent and be baptized . . . in the name of Jesus Christ for the forgiveness of sins. And you will receive the gift of the Holy Spirit" (see also 1 Corinthians 12:13). And third, baptism ties into forgiveness. In Acts 22:16 God's messenger Ananias gives this instruction to Paul: "be baptized and wash your sins away, calling on his name." When Peter writes a letter, he says, "and this water symbolizes baptism that now saves you also—not the removal of dirt from the body but the pledge of a clear conscience toward God. It saves you by the resurrection of Jesus Christ" (1 Peter 3:21).

Baptism does something when we are baptized, but baptism does more than that.

Baptism Keeps on Doing

The reason why Christ triumphs in us over Sin, Flesh, Satan, and Death—each is an agent at work to demolish us—is because we are baptized. Like the Energizer bunny, baptism keeps on working in us. Baptism *continues to **do** death to sin and to **do** life to righteousness.*

Baptism and Death

I suspect the Powerful appealed to the magnificence of God's grace (6:1), and it would not surprise anyone who has participated in a church to learn that some of them were overdoing it with sins. It will also not surprise anyone that others in the church had some words to say about the sins of other Christians. Paul's solution was not more law, more Moses, more observance. Paul counters magnifying sin with a theology of baptism that affirms the grace of God transforming gentile believers into God-fearing and God-honoring and God-loving and God-obeying people. At work in Paul's mission are some who think a gospel for the gentiles that does not require a commitment to observing the law will lead eventually to an immoral gentile life. Paul believes baptism and the Spirit are agents of God's grace to transform a person. The law did not, is not, and will not be able to do that. One detects his concern with the Weak imposing law on the Strong once again. And, once again, he returns to the Q&A approach. Four questions appear in 6:1–2 (bold faced above).

In our baptism we die to sin (6:2–4). Baptism *does* death. In baptism we are united with the baptism of Christ. In his baptism he died on the cross. He entered into the realm of death in order to slay the power of death, which itself is empowered by sin. When we are baptized, we die with Christ who put sin to death. Paul also says "our old self" or "the old human" was itself "crucified with him." Even more, this occurs "so that the body ruled by sin might be done away with" (6:6). In traditional terms, then, Paul believes baptism is not just about an initial forgiveness of sins but is also about what is called "sanctification," or becoming holy and devoted to God in an increasing measure. The one who has died with Christ, that is, been baptized, "has been set free from sin" (6:7). So, in baptism we die in his death to sin. If we live our baptism, we cease sinning because baptism *does* death.

Paul believes in repetition so he says the same thing in a number of ways: "count yourselves dead to sin" and "do not let sin reign in your mortal body" and don't surrender "any part of yourself to sin" because "sin shall no longer be your master" (6:11–14). All of these expressions reveal what baptism *does*.

Baptism and Life

Jesus' baptism was not just a baptism into death but a baptism into resurrection, which means on the other side of death we are raised to a "new life" so we can "live" a new creation life in the power of the Spirit (6:4). The baptized are "set free from sins" (6:7) because they live a resurrection life (6:8). As the life Jesus lives is to God, so we have new life to live with God (6:10).

This new life of baptism's freedom from sin happens "because you are not under the law, but under grace" (6:14). Baptism into the resurrection ushers a human being—Jew or gentile, man or woman, slave or free—into the grace-empowered Christ line. Baptism *does* new life.

A thesis line for Paul then is "count yourselves dead to sin but alive to God in Christ Jesus" (6:11). The foundation for that thesis line is that the believer is summoned, from her baptism on, into living the life of Jesus in the here and now. It is a life of dying to sin and living to what is right. It is not a list of Do's and Don't's but is instead being plunged and soaked into the life of Christ. Baptism *does* a life of righteousness, that is, of being made right with God and doing the right thing.

Questions for Reflection and Application

1. Why should we *not* go all-in on sin, since that would allow God to increase grace?

2. What are three things baptism does when we are first baptized?

3. Why are baptism and the Spirit more important for gentile converts than obeying the law?

4. What role does baptism play in our sanctification?

5. If you have been baptized, what was your view of baptism at the time? How is your understanding of baptism different now? If you have not been baptized, would you like to be?

AGENT SIN, AGENT LIFE, AND REDEMPTIVE PEACE

Romans 6:15–23

[15] *What then?*

Shall we sin because we are not under the law but under grace?

By no means! [16] *Don't you know that when you offer yourselves to someone as obedient slaves, you are slaves of the one you obey—whether you are slaves to sin, which leads to death, or to obedience, which leads to righteousness?* [17] *But thanks be to God that, though you used to be slaves to sin, you have come to obey from your heart the pattern of teaching that has now claimed your allegiance.* [18] *You have been set free from sin and have become slaves to righteousness.*

[19] *I am using an example from everyday life because of your human limitations. Just as you used to offer yourselves as slaves to impurity and to ever-increasing wickedness, so now offer yourselves as slaves to righteousness leading to holiness.* [20] *When you were slaves to sin, you were free from the control of righteousness.*

[21] *What benefit did you reap at that time from the things you are now ashamed of?*

Those things result in death! [22] *But now that you have been set free from sin and have become slaves of God, the benefit you reap leads to holiness, and the result is eternal life.* [23] *For the wages of sin is death, but the gift of God is eternal life in Christ Jesus our Lord.*

Christian life words clarify how God works in us toward redemptive peace. God relentlessly loves us and gives grace to us in spite of our sinfulness. In Christ. That love, which opens up to us in faith and baptism, defeats death and launches an entirely new creation for all those in Christ. This new life empowers both the Powerful and the Powerless to leave the line of Adam and walk in the line of Christ. Paul knows churches, he knows gentile believers, he knows Jewish believers, and he knows that something sinister works in all of us to do the wrong thing. Like stereotyping the other with labels that stick and wound. So sinister is this something that we can add two new expressions to the vocabulary of the Christian life: Agent Sin and Agent Life.

Phoebe will ask her listeners three more questions in our passage (in bold above), but they are all variants on the question asked in 6:1. Someone has countered Paul's gospel and his approach to the right kind of life before God by accusing him of teaching such a load of grace that people are being encouraged to sin. Some of the Powerful loved his approach while some of the Powerless were repulsed. I hear similar worries and accusations in our day. Some push grace so hard they mistakenly state that, if you give grace the right emphasis, you will eventually sound like an *antinomian*, or someone who teaches moral recklessness. Paul would say the same thing to them as he said to the Romans: Never! We remind you that what Paul is saying here derives from his missionary experience where he was constantly accused of abandoning the law and sound morality.

The best understandings of Romans keep the big picture in mind. Otherwise we easily lose our way. The diagram below portrays the big picture. The diagram reveals the formation of two cultures, a toxic one and a healthy one. One is Flesh and Sin and Death and the other is Spirit and Righteousness and Life. Culture, it must be said over and over, cannot be engineered except by a tyrant, which then is not a culture but coercive control. Genuine cultures form from humans making free decisions. Cultures, once formed, become Agents with a kind of power that shapes humans to fit into that culture. If those humans make good decisions, healthy cultures grow; if they make bad decisions, toxic cultures grow.

Paul knows that a life of sinning and trespassing God's ways will promote, nurture, and then solidify, both in a person and in a church, into Sin as an Agent. That is, Sin becomes something alive and well and acting against us. Agent Sin then works down upon us to promote more sinning and eventually can become powerful enough to constrain our behaviors into the ways of sin. Addictions are like this. Paul also knows a that a redemptive alternative—an ongoing pattern of church people doing the right things: trusting, obeying, living in the Spirit, following Jesus—has the capacity to create an entirely different culture in each of us and in us as a body. One in which Life becomes an Agent that, too, works down upon us to do more good. Thus, Agent Life is strengthened, and our internal culture becomes more consistent with the way of Christ into which we were baptized (Croasmun, *Emergence of Sin*).

Choose Your Lord

Paul describes Agent Sin and Agent Life as masters. Any human under their reign become slaves to that Agent. One chooses to be a slave either to sin and death or to obedience

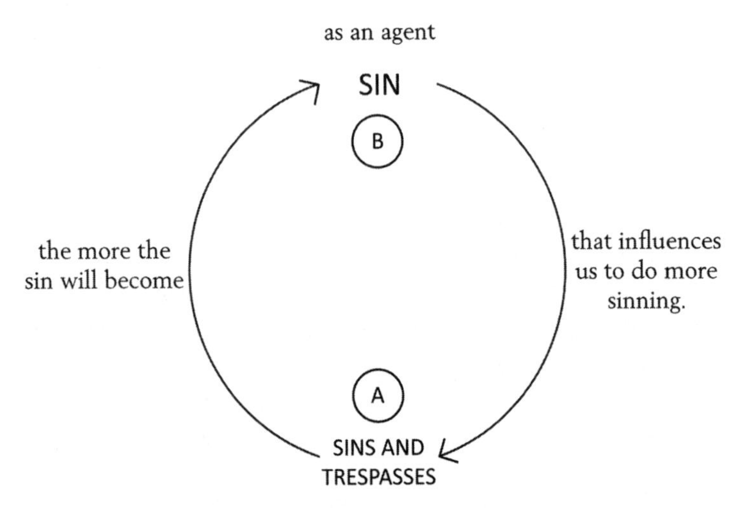
as an agent
SIN
B
that influences
us to do more
sinning.
A
SINS AND
TRESPASSES
The more we live here
the more the
sin will become

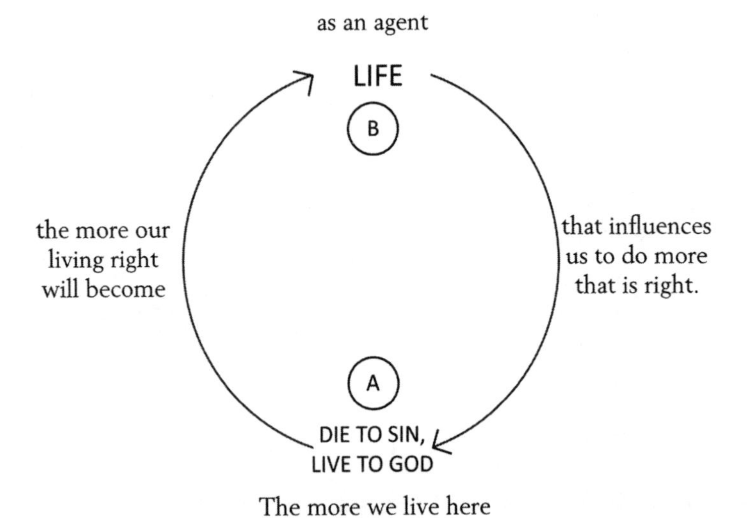
as an agent
LIFE
B
that influences
us to do more
that is right.
A
DIE TO SIN,
LIVE TO GOD
The more we live here
the more our
living right
will become

and righteousness (6:16). The terms Paul uses for choosing begins with their former life, hence "used to be." And the terms for the present life are "obey from your heart" and "claimed your allegiance" (6:17). Describing the life-long growth in the Christian life requires more than one term.

They have handed themselves over to become God's slaves to what is right. That he chose slavery as his image for the Christian life requires a special sensitivity. We are nearly 2,000 years removed from Rome's imperious domination that turned many free persons into slaves to exploit for profit. An enslaved person then and now is a person who is owned and exploited by those with the power to own bodies. Paul's world was saturated with slaves, and some estimate as many as 33% of people in the Roman empire were slaves. While Paul at times transcends slavery with his theme of unity of all as siblings in Christ (Galatians 3:28; Colossians 4:1; Philemon), he does not deconstruct slavery. It took centuries, too many, for humans to perceive and then legislate against slavery for the evil and injustice that it is. Having said that, Paul wants his readers to perceive a kind of moral slavery: either to sin or to grace, life, and righteousness.

The irony is that those who are baptized into Christ's death and resurrection have been *emancipated* from sin-slavery for a freedom in righteousness-slavery (6:18). Furthermore there's a deeper irony here. These believers are called to choose their master, something nearly unheard of in Rome's slave systems.

Two Lords, Two Destinies

As anyone knows (6:19a), one's lord determines one's destiny. There are two options, one under Agent Sin and the other under Agent Life. The two unfold line by line in 6:19–23. The last line tells two stories for two destinies in two short, crisp clauses:

> For the wages of sin is death,
> but the gift of God is eternal life in Christ Jesus our
> Lord (6:23).

Sin leads to death, but God's grace-gift leads to eternal life—and all this is in and because of what Jesus Christ has done for us (summarized in 5:12–21).

What he means by "sin" comes to expression in "impurity" and *lawlessness leading to lawlessness* (6:19; NIV: "ever-increasing wickedness) and being "free from the control of righteousness" (6:20) and of things they were "now ashamed of" (6:21). One thinks here of Romans 1:18–32 again. Such was the gentile life of idolatry they knew in the Adam line (5:12–21), but Adam's line is headed not to life but to "death" (6:16, 21, 23). Sarah Lancaster rightly reminds us that these behaviors transcend what individuals do. They are systems that become cultures that coerce us to conform (Lancaster, *Romans*, 116–117). Agent Sin and Agent Life are culture makers.

The impact of God's grace-gift of redemption is the mirror opposite of the "wages of sin." Thus, instead of being slaves to sins they are now in the Christ line. They now serve God "to righteousness leading to holiness" or utter surrender and devotion to God (6:19, 22), and the results are holiness (6:19, 22), righteousness (6:16), and eternal life (6:22, 23). Choose, then, Agent Life.

Paul captures in Romans 5–8 how to live as a Christian in Rome in the first century when there are divisions among believers. Redemption transforms humans from a life swamped by sin into a life empowered by the Spirit so they can walk in peace, in love, in doing what is right, and in holiness. Christians are called to surrender themselves to God, through Christ, in the power of the Spirit, and the grace of God will empower them to live a new life. The effort of the Christian life is ironically the effort of surrendering to God.

Questions for Reflection and Application

1. How does Sin become an Agent?

2. How does Life become an Agent?

3. How does Paul handle slavery, freedom, and choice in this passage?

4. What are some differences between the culture Sin coerces and the culture Life creates?

5. When have you experienced Sin feeling like an Agent that has control over you? What does freedom and Life in Christ feel like to you by comparison?

FOR FURTHER READING

Matthew Croasmun, *The Emergence of Sin: The Cosmic Tyrant in Romans* (New York: Oxford University Press, 2017). The paragraph at the end of which I mention this book is dependent on Croasmun.

LAW AND REDEMPTIVE PEACE

Romans 7:1–6

[1] Do you not know, brothers and sisters—for I am speaking to those who know the law—that the law has authority over someone only as long as that person lives?

[2] For example, by law a married woman is bound to her husband as long as he is alive, but if her husband dies, she is released from the law that binds her to him. [3] So then, if she has sexual relations with another man while her husband is still alive, she is called an adulteress. But if her husband dies, she is released from that law and is not an adulteress if she marries another man.

[4] So, my brothers and sisters, you also died to the law through the body of Christ, that you might belong to another, to him who was raised from the dead, in order that we might bear fruit for God. [5] For when we were in the realm of the flesh, the sinful passions aroused by the law were at work in us, so that we bore fruit for death. [6] But now, by dying to what once bound us, we have been released from the law so that we serve in the new way of the Spirit, and not in the old way of the written code.

One more question opens chapter seven. We need to remind ourselves that Paul was accused by the Weak or

Powerless (and by opponents still in Jerusalem; see Galatians 2:11–14) of rejecting the law of God, or at least diminishing it. His opponents contend that his diminishing of law observance for gentile converts will lead gentile believers down the slippery slope to immoralities on top of sins. Paul counters that the graces of baptism transform gentiles and Jews into God-loving, others-loving agents of redemptive peace. Or at least they should. (He knows they don't always. So do we.)

The Law of Marriage

To open chapter seven Paul speaks directly to the those who know the law, that is, to the Powerless. He prepped Phoebe to look the Weak in the eye when she performs this chapter. At 6:19 Paul used an analogy drawn from the world of slavery, and now he uses an analogy drawn from the world of law, and he has Moses in mind especially. He has a specific law in mind, namely, the law that binds a man and woman in marriage.

In that law there is a rule about a married woman, or as one could translate it, "a man-attached woman" (7:2). Her relations are restricted to her husband for as long as he is alive. Once he dies, she's free (to remarry or not; 7:3–4). If she has relations with another man while married, she breaks the law of Moses (Exodus 20:14). But if he dies, she's set free from that specific law. This experience with law illustrates the relation of the believer in Jesus to the law.

The Law for the Christ Line

Paul explicitly states that in Christ "you" (7:4) have died to the law. He said this already to the Galatians (2:19). There he said Jewish believers died to the law *through the law,* but in Romans 7 he says Jewish believers experienced death to the law *through the body of Christ* (7:4). Sounds like the baptism of 6:1–14, right? Union with Christ means they can "belong to another," that is to Christ. Union with Christ challenges their former union with the law.

He urges them now to *think of their past* but to think of it in light of new life in Christ. When the Powerless were still unbelievers they were in the Adam line under Agent Sin, that is "in the flesh" (7:5). The law system provoked them to sin and, as he has said more than once already, sin leads to death. Notice that Paul is saying that "the dominion of sin and the dominion of the law constitute the same power sphere" (Hoyt, "Romans," 260).

Which leads to the alternative system, the Christ line and Agent Life. Union with Christ meant these Jewish believers died "to what once bound us" (the law), and death to the law spells out emancipation "from the law" (as the woman was set free when her husband died). Not so they can do whatever they want—remember the accusations Paul constantly faced. No, so these new believers can "serve in the new way of the Spirit" and not in the way of the law (7:6).

Paul does not abolish the law, just as Jesus did not (Matthew 5:17–20). No, as Jesus reinterpreted the law in accordance with the arrival of the king and his kingdom, so Paul takes this one step further. The moral standard of the law of Moses becomes do-able under Agent Life in the Christ line but only *in the Spirit's newness and freshness* (7:6). Paul will tell them in chapter eight that the "righteous requirement of the law" will be made complete for believers as they live "according to the Spirit" (8:4). Which means Paul is not against the law at all. He's for it. Those who live in the Spirit do all the law wanted and more.

Something new requires something more. The new age in Christ expects more of those who are in Christ. Their more comes from the Spirit.

Questions for Reflection and Application

1. What were the fears of the Weak/Powerless about Paul's teaching on the law?

2. How are human relationships with law and with Christ like marriage?

3. How do you think those who advocate for the law Moses as a vital part of the Christian life will respond to what Paul argues here? Try to think from their point of view. What will they say in their own defense?

4. What does God expect of people after they are freed from the law?

5. When you think of your past in light of your new life in Christ, what comes to mind?

EGO AND REDEMPTIVE PEACE

Romans 7:7–25

[7] *What shall we say, then?*

Is the law sinful?

Certainly not! Nevertheless, I would not have known what sin was had it not been for the law. For I would not have known what coveting really was if the law had not said, "You shall not covet." [8] *But sin, seizing the opportunity afforded by the commandment, produced in me every kind of coveting. For apart from the law, sin was dead.* [9] *Once I was alive apart from the law; but when the commandment came, sin sprang to life and I died.* [10] *I found that the very commandment that was intended to bring life actually brought death.* [11] *For sin, seizing the opportunity afforded by the commandment, deceived me, and through the commandment put me to death.* [12] *So then, the law is holy, and the commandment is holy, righteous and good.*

[13] *Did that which is good, then, become death to me?*

By no means! Nevertheless, in order that sin might be recognized as sin, it used what is good to bring about my death, so that through the commandment sin might become utterly sinful.

[14] *We know that the law is spiritual; but I am unspiritual, sold as a slave to sin.* [15] *I do not understand what I do. For what I want to do I do not do, but what I hate I do.* [16] *And if I do what I do not*

want to do, I agree that the law is good. [17] As it is, it is no longer I myself who do it, but it is sin living in me. [18] For I know that good itself does not dwell in me, that is, in my sinful nature. For I have the desire to do what is good, but I cannot carry it out. [19] For I do not do the good I want to do, but the evil I do not want to do—this I keep on doing. [20] Now if I do what I do not want to do, it is no longer I who do it, but it is sin living in me that does it.

[21] So I find this law at work: Although I want to do good, evil is right there with me. [22] For in my inner being I delight in God's law; [23] but I see another law at work in me, waging war against the law of my mind and making me a prisoner of the law of sin at work within me. [24] What a wretched man I am! Who will rescue me from this body that is subject to death? [25] Thanks be to God, who delivers me through Jesus Christ our Lord!

So then, I myself in my mind am a slave to God's law, but in my sinful nature a slave to the law of sin.

Let me be like Paul and ask a bundle of questions. But I ask who is this Ego, or "I," of Romans 7?

Paul?

Who is this "I" Paul writes about?
Is it Paul himself with I telling us Paul's personal story?
And, if the I is Paul, is it his pre-Christian experience under the law or his post-Christian experience?

Not Paul?

Or does he represent someone else with this "I"?
And if so, who does the "I" represent?
Adam (and Eve)?
Jews?
The Weak?

The Strong?
All believers?
All humans?

If this confuses you, please sit with me in the seats for the Confused or Not So Sure. Scholars have argued about the Ego of Romans 7 for a long time. What no one can dispute is that "I" gives the passage a directness and a sense of a personal testimony. One has a hard time not believing a personal testimony like this. Paul knew what he was doing using Ego in this passage.

I'm going to do my best to identify the Ego of Romans 7.

Identifying the Ego

A passage in Philippians makes it almost impossible to think of the Ego in Romans 7 as Paul's own experience—especially his pre-Christian experience as an observant Jew under the law of Moses. In Philippians Paul writes, and I reformat to slow down our reading:

> For it is we who are the circumcision, we who serve God by his Spirit, who boast in Christ Jesus, and who put no confidence in the flesh—though I myself have reasons for such confidence. If someone else thinks they have reasons to put confidence in the flesh, I have more:
>
> 1. circumcised on the eighth day,
> 2. of the people of Israel,
> 3. of the tribe of Benjamin,
> 4. a Hebrew of Hebrews;
> 5. in regard to the law, a Pharisee;
> 6. as for zeal, persecuting the church;
> 7. as for righteousness based on the law, faultless (3:3–6).

Numbers 1–4 describe Paul's confidence in his Jewishness. Numbers 5–7 detail Paul's confidence in his obedience of the law and of his lack of a haunting guilt before God for sins. Take a clear-eyed look at #7: "as for righteousness based on the law" he says he was "faultless." The Ego of Romans 7 comes off as someone tortured under the law. When we compare the clean-conscience and confidence of Philippians 3 above with the tortured Ego of Romans 7, we have to conclude Romans 7's Ego cannot then describe Paul's own sense of his pre-Christian experience under the law.

So who is it? Someone else. Who? If we recall the opening to chapter seven we most likely have our answer: those who know the law (7:1–6). Which means Jews, better yet, Jewish Christians, better yet, the Weak or Powerless of Romans 14–15 and especially their representative Judge in Romans 2.

Paul uses the "I" in Romans 7 to create a character, which we often refer to as creating a "speech in character." It was common in the ancient world. Paul's audience in Rome would have immediately recognized what Paul was doing. By using "I," Paul gives the person some character and personality, and creating the character permits Paul to peer inside the heart and mind of the person to describe what it's like being that person. This Ego character, who is a Christian, believes the way to live the Christian life is to adopt observance of the law of Moses. Which is to say, the most likely identity of the Ego of Romans 7 can be found in the Judge of Romans 2.

Please notice the absence of Spirit and redemption in Romans 7. The absence of terms like Spirit and redemption provides a valuable clue for identifying the Ego of Romans 7. Paul knows one cannot live the way God wants without living in the Spirit on the basis of redemption in Christ. So the Ego of Romans 7 is a seriously misguided person: a believer in Christ who ignores the transforming powers of the Spirit by returning to the law alone as the guide for discipleship.

Three Insights for the Ego Life

Paul wants them to learn what the law actually is designed by God to accomplish. It doesn't transform a person, God does. One can't do the law on one's own, but the Spirit can empower us to be faithful (8:4). So, the entire backdrop for reading Romans 7:7–25 is to know the way to live out our baptism into the life of Christ is not by following the law but by living in the Spirit. In Romans 7 Paul attempts to demolish the law observance approach to life in Christ.

First, an insight about *the law.* God designed the law to expose our sinfulness. Paul picks on "covet," but the term can be translated to desire or excessive desire and ambition (see pp. 144–145). The Ego learns from the law that desire is contrary to God's way (7:7).

Second, an insight about *Agent Sin and the law.* Agent Sin seizes the law against desire and pushes the Ego to want the freedom of reckless desire (7:8). Paul even says the law on its own accomplishes nothing without Agent Sin. Agent Sin manipulates God's gift of the law to generate sin in a person and lead them to death (7:9–11). This second point is the emphasis of Paul also in 7:13, where Paul says the law turned ordinary "sin" into the "utterly sinful" or "hyperbolically sinful." That is, it exaggerates the reality and nature of sin. It turns peccadillos into capital offenses.

Time for a brief clarification by Paul because, as he has learned in every synagogue where he preached Jesus as Messiah, he has been accused of skirting on the edge of something close to heresy by diminishing Moses. The law, he affirms, is not the problem. God gave the law; what God gives cannot be the problem. It's "holy" and "righteous" and "good" (7:12). What Paul means is that the law is God's expression of his will for his people, but the law does not have the power to transform humans into law-observant, victorious, flourishing believers. It can write an expose of humans, but it cannot redeem them or transform them. Only redemption in Christ and life in the Spirit can do that.

Third, an insight about *the law and Agent Sin and the Ego*. The law alone is not the problem. *The Ego becomes the problem because it unites itself with Agent Sin*. Read 7:14–24 carefully because Paul wants the Weak to see that their theory of discipleship just won't work. It can't. The law can't do what they want it to do. Not because it's bad but because a human has a corrupted Ego. The Weak need to see that the Ego is "unspiritual" and is "sold as a slave to sin" and does not "understand." Instead, what it wants to do it doesn't do and what it doesn't want to do it does. Not just the Ego, but Agent Sin "living in me" (7:17) in a reality Paul calls "flesh" (NIV has "sinful nature" for flesh in 7:18). So much so that the Powerless Judge represented in the Ego wants to do what is "good" but just can't pull it off, which he says a few times again in 7:21–23. So knotted together are sin, the Ego, and the law that Paul gasps "What a wretched person Ego is" (7:24; my translation).

Resolving the Ego

The Ego has been defeated by Agent Sin in the heart of a human. So much so that Paul gasps out a question, "Who will rescue the Ego from this death-destined body?" (my translation, 7:24). His gasped question sets up an answer we will discover in Romans 8, where Paul puts on the final touches of how to live as someone who has been baptized into Christ's life, death, and resurrection. The Ego can only be rescued "through Jesus Christ our Lord" (7:25).

Paul describes the Ego life, but he cannot now be accused of degrading or diminishing the law. Rather he reframes law observance, first in verse twenty-five and then fully in chapter eight. His summary conclusion then is "in the Ego's mind the Ego is a slave to God's law" but "in the Ego's flesh the Ego is a slave to a law of Agent Sin" (7:25). Remember where chapter seven began again: with the one who knows the law dying to the law (7:1–6). The one who has died to the law but wants to revive the law is the one Phoebe must turn her eyes to as she reads this chapter.

The tensions in Rome about how best to live as followers of Jesus requires a careful understanding of law and of Ego. When we add those to terms like God's love and Adam and Christ and Flesh, the Christian life begins to come into clearer view, a bit like my almost daily experience of spotting a duck on the lake or bird in a tree, pulling out my field glasses, adjusting them on the duck or bird and, boom!, the identity become clear. Paul forms a compelling network of terms. The next two nearly complete the network's energy.

Questions for Reflection and Application

1. How does Paul's confidence in his Jewishness in Philippians contrast with the I of Romans 7?

2. What do the Weak/Powerless of Rome have in common with the I in Romans 7?

3. Why is the Spirit so important to our life of Christ?

4. How do law and Sin and Ego work together to create a problem?

5. When have you felt the kind of desperation the Ego character expresses in verses 15–19? What helped you in that battle?

SPIRIT, FLESH, AND REDEMPTIVE PEACE

Romans 8:1–17

[1] Therefore, there is now no condemnation for those who are in Christ Jesus, [2] because through Christ Jesus the law of the Spirit who gives life has set you free from the law of sin and death. [3] For what the law was powerless to do because it was weakened by the flesh, God did by sending his own Son in the likeness of sinful flesh to be a sin offering. And so he condemned sin in the flesh, [4] in order that the righteous requirement of the law might be fully met in us, who do not live according to the flesh but according to the Spirit.

[5] Those who live according to the flesh have their minds set on what the flesh desires; but those who live in accordance with the Spirit have their minds set on what the Spirit desires. [6] The mind governed by the flesh is death, but the mind governed by the Spirit is life and peace. [7] The mind governed by the flesh is hostile to God; it does not submit to God's law, nor can it do so. [8] Those who are in the realm of the flesh cannot please God.

[9] You, however, are not in the realm of the flesh but are in the realm of the Spirit, if indeed the Spirit of God lives in you. And if anyone does not have the Spirit of Christ, they do not belong to Christ. [10] But if Christ is in you, then even though your body is subject to death because of sin, the Spirit gives life because of

righteousness. [11] *And if the Spirit of him who raised Jesus from the dead is living in you, he who raised Christ from the dead will also give life to your mortal bodies because of his Spirit who lives in you.*

[12] *Therefore, brothers and sisters, we have an obligation—but it is not to the flesh, to live according to it.* [13] *For if you live according to the flesh, you will die; but if by the Spirit you put to death the misdeeds of the body, you will live.*

[14] *For those who are led by the Spirit of God are the children of God.* [15] *The Spirit you received does not make you slaves, so that you live in fear again; rather, the Spirit you received brought about your adoption to sonship. And by him we cry, "Abba, Father."* [16] *The Spirit himself testifies with our spirit that we are God's children.* [17] *Now if we are children, then we are heirs—heirs of God and co-heirs with Christ, if indeed we share in his sufferings in order that we may also share in his glory.*

Sometimes our remote control doesn't work. Kris always says, "Check the batteries." At other times the light in our bathroom won't come on when we flip the switch. Kris always says, "Check the trip on the outlet." Sometimes the lawn mower or the snow blower won't start, or they stop in the middle of the task. I always say to myself, "Check the gas." These three hold one thing in common: they are the fuel needed to produce power. The fuel of the Christian life is neither a spiritual discipline nor an activity. The fuel is the Spirit of God, God's empowering presence at work in us (Fee, *Empowering Presence*).

God has filled our tank, as it were; God has opened the lines for the electricity to flow. Our response is to receive, to be open, to be filled (Ephesians 5:18). The Spirit becomes the internal power for us to defeat the flesh, to overcome sin, and to conquer death. In Rome, those victories are over labeling and stereotyping others in a way that "others" them. The flipside of these victories reveals that the Spirit *implements* in us what Christ *has already accomplished* for us. Any approach to Christian living that avoids or diminishes God's empowering presence shuts down the power at work in us.

Paul poses the Spirit of God in today's reading against the Flesh, now visible in the tensions in Rome.

Spirit

Jesus' operative word for what we call Christian living was "following" or "discipleship." In Paul's mission to the gentiles, he adapted Jesus' terms to a new world. Paul's vision of following Jesus was to *live in the Spirit*. The Spirit empowers the lights for Christians.

Paul mentions "spirit" almost 160 times in his letters. Most refer to the Holy Spirit, some to the human spirit, and a few of them are too close to call. Which gives us an insight into what God wants us to know: God's Spirit and the human spirit are made for one another. The Spirit awakens, illumines, and renews us so we can become the person God designed us to be. So we can become Christlike, conformed to the image of the Son of God (8:29). We are Spirit-awakened spirits (and bodies) empowered to walk in the fruit of the Spirit exercising the gifts of the Spirit as we live the life of the Spirit.

The connection of Spirit to human spirit deserves a little more explanation. Take the word "spiritual" as in spiritual gifts (1 Corinthians 12–14): when spirit is connected to gift it becomes a Spirit-prompted gift of God to the church, so even "spiritual" gift with a lower case "s" falls short. The same is the case in Romans 7:4 when it says the "law is spiritual." We could translate it "Spirit-given." But what about 1 Corinthians 2:13, which translated literally reads "discerning *spirituals in spirituals*." The NIV translates by adding the two underlined words to make it clear: "explaining *spiritual realities* with *Spirit-taught words*." We could also translate it "Spirit matters co-discerned by a Spirit-person." Our *inability* not to know for sure if one or both of these spirit-words is the divine Spirit or a human spirit unlocks a secret to who we are: Spirit-receptive spirits.

Flesh

Another important human reality has the capacity to shut off the electricity or empty the tank of its fuel. As the human spirit is made for God's Spirit, so the *Flesh* forms into a person's local host for Agent Sin. If you read today's passage carefully you see "Spirit" 16 times and "flesh" 12 times. Spirit is in the Christ line under Agent Life, and the flesh is in the Adam line under Agent Sin.

The flesh is the residue of Adam in us as we await the final kingdom of God. We live between the First Advent of Christ and the Second Advent. Living "between the times" means we are both truly redeemed and not yet completely redeemed. We are in Christ but there's some Adam and Eve residue in each of us. Paul calls what remains from the Adam era "Flesh." Yes, the Flesh is connected to the body but the "body" to which it is connected is the body destined for death and destruction, not the body destined for a glorious body fit for the presence of God in the kingdom of God.

So two more vital terms for Christian living are Spirit and Flesh. The former empowers Christian living and the latter *de*powers a human to orient one's existence toward sin and death.

Life in the Spirit

Romans 8 takes our breath away in scope and grandeur. The chapter also opens the door for the Weak and the Strong to view the importance of the Spirit for living victoriously in the community of Jesus in Rome. The Flesh divides; the Spirit unites. The Flesh welcomes only some to the table; the Spirit welcomes all to the table. The Spirit is God's empowering presence that transforms Flesh-y behavior into Spirit-prompted behavior.

A life in the Spirit involves the following five elements.

First, a life in the Spirit *frees us from the law's condemnation* (8:1–4). Those who know the law learn its searing powers to expose our sins. Sins unmask Agent Sin at work in us and remind us again our old standing in the Adam line (see the lists in 5:12–21 at pp. 117–118). Those in the Christ line, however, died to the law in their baptism into Christ's death. They are now alive beyond the law because they are also baptized into Christ's resurrection and the empowering presence of God in the Spirit. Thus, those in Christ are "free from the law of sin and death" (8:2). The law, diminished in power by Sin and Flesh, is "powerless" to redeem us and transform us. Christ accomplishes what the law never accomplishes. This is what God does: "God—sending his own Son in the representation of Sin's Flesh—for Sin also condemned Sin-in-the-Flesh" (8:3, my translation). Because we are in the Flesh, we cannot do the law but, and the Powerless must have loved what comes next, and the Powerful were perhaps a bit disturbed by these words: *in the Spirit* "the righteous requirement of the law might be fully met in us" (8:4). I don't know if you see this, but I think I do: you and I, in the Spirit, are empowered to do *fully* what God has willed for us to do!

Second, the Spirit *clashes with the flesh* (8:5–8). Because the Spirit empowers us to do what God wants, the Flesh goes to battle against us. Flesh-ers do the Flesh life, but Spirit-people do the Spirit life. Here are the polar opposites:

Flesh	vs.	Spirit
Death	vs.	Life
Hostile to God and God's law	vs.	Peace
Cannot please God	vs.	Pleasing to God

Those listening to Phoebe at this point might be murmuring something about what seems like an embattled life. Paul moves on to clarify.

Third, a life in the Spirit *occurs only in Christ* (8:9–11). The baptized are not in the Flesh or standing in the Adam line (5:12–21). They take up a spot in the Christ line and thus they stand and walk and run "in the realm of the Spirit" (8:9). God's Spirit empowers only those who are in the Spirit made possible only in Christ. First Christ, then the Spirit. Paul reminds them of a divine indwelling in two ways in these verses: the Spirit is in us, and Christ is in us (8:9, 10).

Fourth, a life in the Spirit *becomes an obligation to the Spirit life* (8:12–13). Now the condition is spelled out clearly. Believers have an obligation to choose the Spirit life over the Flesh (and Sin and Death) life. The flesh life leads to death; the Spirit life leads to eternal life. There are two ways, and the Weak and the Strong will have to choose which of the ways is for them.

Fifth, a life in the Spirit *regenerates us into God's children* (8:14–17). Life in the Spirit only occurs through the redemption in Christ, and only those led by the Spirit are truly "children of God." The Flesh and Sin and Death systems make humans slaves, but the Spirit re-creates them to children by "adoption." As adopted children of God they have learned to call God "*Abba*, Father."

Paul says something next that must have vexed many believers in his churches. Many wonder if they are God's children; others are tormented by doubt. Paul's pastoral experience revealed to him that the Spirit in them "testifies with our spirit that we are God's children" (8:16). This internal witness is both real and yet also experiential and subjective. One senses this in one's spirit, which is made for the divine Spirit's habitation. Over and over Paul must have told people in his churches how to detect the presence of the Spirit—the Spirit talks to us.

Our chapter divisions are tidy but ancient letters were not. The last verse of today's reading segues to the next section with new terms that set the stage. Two fresh terms here are "heirs" and "suffering," both of which figure into the next section in Romans.

Questions for Reflection and Application

1. How does the Spirit work to fuel or empower our Christian life?

2. What roles do Flesh and Spirit play in the conflict in the Roman house churches?

3. What does it mean for humans to be Spirit-receptive spirits?

4. How does the Spirit work in us to help us in the battle against Flesh and Sin?

5. Consider the work of the Spirit moving people from being slaves to being children. How does this comparison help you understand the Spirit's work?

FOR FURTHER READING

Gordon Fee, *God's Empowering Presence: The Holy Spirit in the Letters of Paul* (Peabody, Mass.: Hendrickson, 1994).

SUFFERING AND REDEMPTIVE PEACE

Romans 8:18–30

[18] I consider that our present sufferings are not worth comparing with the glory that will be revealed in us. [19] For the creation waits in eager expectation for the children of God to be revealed. [20] For the creation was subjected to frustration, not by its own choice, but by the will of the one who subjected it, in hope [21] that the creation itself will be liberated from its bondage to decay and brought into the freedom and glory of the children of God.

[22] We know that the whole creation has been groaning as in the pains of childbirth right up to the present time. [23] Not only so, but we ourselves, who have the firstfruits of the Spirit, groan inwardly as we wait eagerly for our adoption to sonship, the redemption of our bodies. [24] For in this hope we were saved. But hope that is seen is no hope at all. Who hopes for what they already have? [25] But if we hope for what we do not yet have, we wait for it patiently.

[26] In the same way, the Spirit helps us in our weakness. We do not know what we ought to pray for, but the Spirit himself intercedes for us through wordless groans. [27] And he who searches our hearts knows the mind of the Spirit, because the Spirit intercedes for God's people in accordance with the will of God.

[28] And we know that in all things God works for the good of those who love him, who have been called according to his purpose. [29] For those God foreknew he also predestined to be conformed to the image of his Son, that he might be the firstborn among many brothers and sisters. [30] And those he predestined, he also called; those he called, he also justified; those he justified, he also glorified.

The last passage ended with nothing less than a surprising as well as breathtaking approach to suffering. Christian suffering participates in the very life of Christ, that is, his suffering and his resurrection to glory. Paul said, "if indeed we share in his sufferings in order that we may also share in his glory" (8:17). Just why he brought up suffering when he was running back and forth between the terms Flesh and Spirit is not entirely clear. Previously Paul mentioned suffering at 5:3–5, and he connected it to spiritual formation (perseverance, character, hope). In those three verses he sketched the positive growth impact of suffering. Now Paul adds that suffering participates in, and unites us to, Christ's own suffering.

We can learn a more Christian approach to our own suffering by carefully attending to today's passage, but before we can do that, we need to figure out just what is meant by "suffering."

Suffering

Read Romans 8:18–30 carefully and underline or circle or mark every term connected to suffering. Here are the terms I find:

Present suffering (8:18)
Frustration (8:20)
Bondage to decay (8:21)

Groaning (8:22, 23, 26)
Weakness (8:26)

And maybe you marked as I did the "all things" in 8:28 because you wondered if "all things" sums up all the suffering terms he has just used. To know what "suffering" in 8:17 and in 8:18 means we need to look at all these terms. They bring suffering into full view, and our view is macroscopic for sure.

Now add what is said about suffering in 8:35–39, and we can see just what is in view:

Trouble, hardship, persecution, famine, nakedness, danger, sword (8:35)
Death (8:36; from Psalm 44:22)
Death/life, angels/demons, present/future, powers, height/depth, nothing in all creation (8:38–39)

All suffering. Any suffering. Of whatever kind. In between the First and Second Advents, in what Tom Wright calls the "wrinkle of time," humans will experience suffering (Wright, "Romans," 606). Of all sorts. Much of it forms of persecution, but not just persecution.

Suffering in this passage describes the not-yet-fully redeemed creation, churches, and humans—all suffering as they seek to live in the Spirit in a world dominated by Flesh that opposes and resists a Spirit-led life. That is, suffering is the whole human body suffering with the whole lot of humanity, in the whole creation, in the totality of the human experience, because redemption is not yet fully completed. This pertains especially to disabilities, to physical or cognitive conditions that impact a person in her or his social participation. Paul may well have looked at festering wounds on his body or the shackles on his feet in some Roman prison and said, "These are my sufferings because I follow Jesus, and I can see in them the suffering of all creation awaiting God's final, full redemption."

Suffering of some sort is our lot. Because we avail ourselves of modern medicine, which daily grows in its complicated understanding of how the human body works and what can be done to repair and restore it, suffering for us clashes with suffering in Paul's world. Most did not live long. The average age of skeletons found ancient Romans hovered around 30 years old. The lifespan of Romans was considerably unlike ours. And that did not mean 29.5 years of robust health. Slaves suffered from the toils of labor, and diseases ran rampant at times through entire blocks of communities. Add deaths in childbirth and war as well as some unpredictable natural disasters like famines, and the average age at death indicates a harsh reality. Suffering was their way of life, and Paul has a theology of suffering because he's witnessed the realities of suffering in his churches. Nothing rose to the level of the daily experience and routine feelings of the ordinary person in Roman house church than suffering.

He has learned in his own life and pastoral work at least the following four perspectives on suffering.

Walk Ahead with Your Eyes on Complete Liberation

Sufferers want the pain to end. As is the case now so it was then: a promise of future justice rings hollow when that is all one has to offer. To tell women that all abuse will end in the kingdom crushes a sense of hope for justice and change now. To continue singing songs about the end of racism in heaven turns hope into some kind of manipulative trick to keep black Americans under the thumb of white power. These observations must be kept in mind as we turn to Paul's message of redemptive liberation someday.

Sufferings in the present season, Paul tells them, stands no chance against the "glory" that is to come (8:18), but Paul adds color and texture to the term glory with the following: hope (8:20), liberating from enslavement to physical decay (8:21), and freedom (8:21). With one's eyes on radical liberation, one can look suffering in the eyes and take the next step in life.

Paul assigns "bondage to decay" to divine providence. God has subjected creation to "frustration" or, as one might translate it, "creation's impatient expectation" (8:20). But he also attributes its liberation to an act of God, indicated by the passive voice in "will *be liberated*" (by God) (8:21). The common human experience of suffering describes a dimension of God's plan for all creation. That can be a difficult concept to accept when one is going through a sickening display of injustice or death too early or a disability that gets a social label, but Paul speaks in general categories. He would explain unjust violence as the acts of sinful humans dominated by the Flesh, while also stating that ultimately God orders all creation. Paul does not dismiss pain nor pretend it can be tricked by positive thinking. He resists injustices.

But Paul informs us of the biggest perspective of all: "creation [that] waits in eager expectation." Creation cries out for humans to treat it as God's work, not theirs to exploit. God's created order becomes an Agent of hope, and what it hopes for is the apocalyptic revelation of "the children of God" (8:19). What an amazing moment: someday creation will, like the trees in C.S. Lewis' *The Last Battle,* clap and celebrate and sing hallelujahs when the children of God are unveiled as those who will become fully like Christ. The language is wedding-like as the entire audience awaits the appearance of the bride. Accompanying them, all creation will march into the same liberation and glory as the children of God (8:21).

That destiny becomes the fullness of redemptive peace.

Walk Ahead with a Spirit-Prompted Groaning

This hope for cosmic redemption turns all creation into a constant state of a simmering, experiential "groaning" (8:22–23). Our frustrations, our expectations that justice ought to be established, and our God-planted dream to undo our shattered lives because of cancers and heart attacks and violence are legitimated by God's design. God made us to long for what is right and fair and just and good and peaceful and loving and wise. Suffering may be real, but it is not right. Someday your "body" will experience "redemption" and someday your relationships will be healed (8:23).

God's Spirit in our spirit groans and aches and longs for the complete redemption of the body. Our bodies will not be shucked aside like the skins of an ear of corn. The body figures centrally in final redemption. Think about it this way: the Spirit, creation, and the children of God sing a song of groaning in harmony, in parts, all prompted by the providential plan of God. This groaning is "a community lament," like a nursery of women delivering children at the same time (Gorman, *Romans*, 205).

Two more perspectives on suffering now.

Walk Ahead with Your Spirit-Shaped Prayer Life

We not only are instructed to grow up into a worldview that puts suffering in its place as described in today's passage, and it won't happen quickly or easily, but we also learn to discern how to pray and what to pray for (8:26–27). The groaning Spirit guides each of us into perceiving our final desires and hopes. The Spirit takes the inexpressible and unexpressed and turns both into intelligible expressions in God's presence. Not only that, but the Father-God guides the groaning Spirit to guide us to discern what God wants. God created us with an inner need to groan for what God wants. Our groaning participates in the ways of God. Spirit-shaped prayers convert the expectations, hopes, groanings, aches, and longings of humans into the divinely-spoken prayer requests in the throne room of God.

Accept the emotions of groaning as a sign God's work has found a home in you.

Walk Ahead with Your God-Ordained Destiny

We return to the first perspective but this time in a new key. The hope and liberation as God's children is final conformity to the image of Christ (8:28–29). Again, in the midst of suffering, hope can sustain us and grant us the courage to move on. In spite of how popular Romans 8:28 is to so many Christians, the standard translation may overstate. It may be best to translate it as "We know that God co-works all things for good with those who love God." The "all things" are not doing the action here; God is.

Paul does not reach down to some bottom level of commonsense to say "things will be OK ultimately" and neither does he suggest that "all things" is a kind of pantheism at work in the cosmos that eventually swirls things in a good direction. Nor does he push the believers in Rome to think that arc of history will bring justice. Paul talks God here. It is God who is in and under and beside and in front of all things as the divine plan works its purposes. The plan is for the children of God to end up conformed to Jesus himself. That result has an inevitability about it because the terms are linked: from predestination to calling to justification to glorification. We are back to the "glory" term of 8:18, now making clear what that glory is. The image of God impressed onto Adam and Eve, marred by sin, will be set free to become what it should be: Christlikeness.

Sacraments of Glory

I don't know that kind of suffering you may be experiencing. Maybe we can receive ordinary sufferings like sicknesses and the inevitability of death, or the kind of suffering that comes from persecution and dangers and wars, as sacraments of final glory. That is, maybe we can see through our sufferings the way many Christians see through icons or paintings or creation or love or purposes in life into the heart of God's design for us and for the world. Maybe those specific sufferings can become for us a vision of what we will someday be. Liberated, redeemed, glorified. Marilynne Robinson, in her wonderful little novel *Gilead*, puts suffering in these words: "I heard a man say once that Christians worship sorrow. That is by no means true. But we do believe there is a sacred mystery in it, it's fair to say" and her old pastor continues with "I believe there is a dignity in sorrow simply because it is God's good pleasure that there should be. He is forever raising up those who are brought low" (Robinson, *Gilead*, 137).

In the next passage we turn to the final word in the network of words about the kind of redemptive peace that has the potential to turn the divisions in Rome into a loving unity.

Questions for Reflection and Application

1. How do the increase in medical science and the resulting reduction in human suffering impact our understanding of Paul's teachings on suffering?

2. Consider this shifted translation of Romans 8:28: "We know that God co-works all things for good with those who love God." How does this affect your understanding of the verse?

3. What role might suffering have played in the conflicts in the Roman churches?

4. How can we balance our hope for future liberation in the new creation with our work for justice now?

5. In what ways could you see suffering in your life as a sacrament?

FOR FURTHER READING

Marilynne Robinson, *Gilead* (New York: Farrar, Strauss and Giroux, 2004).

VICTORY AND REDEMPTIVE PEACE

Romans 8:31–39

[31] *What, then, shall we say in response to these things?*

If God is for us, who can be against us?

[32] *He who did not spare his own Son, but gave him up for us all—how will he not also, along with him, graciously give us all things?*

[33] *Who will bring any charge against those whom God has chosen?*

It is God who justifies.

[34] *Who then is the one who condemns?*

No one. Christ Jesus who died—more than that, who was raised to life—is at the right hand of God and is also interceding for us.

[35] *Who shall separate us from the love of Christ?*

Shall trouble or hardship or persecution or famine or nakedness or danger or sword?

[36] *As it is written:*

> *"For your sake we face death all day long;*
> *we are considered as sheep to be slaughtered."*

> [37] *No, in all these things we are more than conquerors through him who loved us.* [38] *For I am convinced that neither death nor life, neither angels nor demons, neither the present nor the future, nor any powers,* [39] *neither height nor depth, nor anything else in all creation, will be able to separate us from the love of God that is in Christ Jesus our Lord.*

The entire letter of Romans puts together Paul's wisdom learned in gospel mission. Paul's optimistic expressions about hope and God's victory and the kingdom of God and the presence of the Spirit and the lordship of Jesus—and that his gospel is God's planned message for the whole world—must have inspired his church people to believe life was good and getting better. For two decades he has been evangelizing Asia Minor and Greece, and hope runs right through each day in those two decades. But reality disconfirmed so much of that hope. One concern, it not criticism, Paul heard many times was, "Why, if we are God's people, if we are doing what is right, if God is among us, if the Spirit is transforming us, if Jesus is the world's true Lord, are we suffering?"

His answers grew from the roots of his own sufferings, and we need to look at those now.

Paul's Wisdom from His Own Suffering

When Paul speaks of suffering as he did in the previous passage (see pp. 170–171), he knew the experience. Please read this passage slowly and carefully. If you want, imagine where his body was marked with wounds and scars by persecutions. I have added numbers to show the variety of his sufferings, and if we knew precise details the number 28 could easily be added to.

> I have worked much harder, [1] been in prison more frequently, [2] been flogged more severely, [3] and been exposed to death again and again. 24 [4–8] Five times I received from the Jews the forty lashes minus one. 25 [9–11] Three times I was beaten with rods, [12] once I was pelted with stones, [13–15] three times I was shipwrecked, [16] I spent a night and a day in the open sea, 26 I have been constantly on the move. [17] I have been in danger from rivers, [18] in danger from bandits, [19] in danger from my fellow Jews, [20] in danger from Gentiles; [21] in danger in the city, [22] in danger in the country, [23] in danger at sea; [24] and in danger from false believers. 27 [25] I have labored and toiled and [26] have often gone without sleep; [27] I have known hunger and thirst and have often gone without food; [28] I have been cold and naked (2 Corinthians 11:23b–27).

Paul knew sufferings. He surely informed believers that the first experience of gospel suffering can be the toughest because it turns from some theory they have heard about to an emotional, physical, social reality. Paul seems to have gotten used to suffering, so used to it he could examine it from the outside looking in.

Someone who has started a business from scratch can inform the new start up about best procedure. Someone who has mothered children can help the new mother the most. Someone who has pastored for decades can be the wisest person in the room when talking to younger pastors. In other words, listen to experience from the sages if you want to be wise. So, the one who has suffered as much as Paul suffered can instruct the Roman believers—both the Powerful and especially the Powerless (since Paul, too, was a Jew)—how to think about their own suffering.

Which he has just done in the previous passage and now elaborates into one of the most popular passages in the entire New Testament.

Paul's Wisdom for All Suffering

The passage can be cut in two, one part dealing with "God's got this" and the second part with "God's got us."

God's Got This

Paul's second question in the NIV is rhetorical:
"If God is for us, who can be against us?"
Answer: No one.
That question turns over slightly onto its side with:
[If the God of all gave his Son for us] "how will he not also, along with [giving] him, *grace us with* all things?" (My revision of the NIV.)
Answer: Certainly!
A slight turn again becomes:
"Who will bring any charge against" us?
Answer: Nobody!
Another turn for another adjustment to the original question:
"Who then is the one who condemns?"
Answer: No one!

Two footings stand unmoved under these questions: God is for us, and Christ has died and been raised for us and is now interceding for us. The best news for anyone suffering, at least anyone who can do nothing about it, is that God's got this!

God's Got Us

God's not just got this, but God's got us in strong, safe hands. Nothing can separate us from God's unconditional, unwavering, relentless, and adjusting love. Read Romans 5:1–5 that started this middle section of Romans (5–8). In that first passage in the section Paul connected suffering and God's love, and that's what he does now to end this middle section of Romans. But this time in an exultant flurry of questions and expectations and claims.

Paul turns to what sufferers know from experience ("trouble . . . sword"; 8:35) the experiences that tempt them to walk from the faith and turn their back on Jesus. But Paul learned from his own suffering to comprehend and reframe suffering with two strategies: (1) he is united with Christ in his sufferings and (2) he will in the end find justice. The united with Christ theme, beginning at a believer's baptism (6:1–14), finds footings in Psalm 44's admission that those faithful to God at times know that they are like "sheep to be slaughtered" (Romans 8:36).

Sufferings of all sorts can be turned on their head when one rethinks them through the reality of the resurrection of Jesus. That's why Paul says, "in all these things we"—those who love God—are more than conquerors" (8:37). Or, we "super conquer" in Christ the afflictions we bear prior to the final kingdom.

No one can condemn us, no one can pry us loose from redemption in Christ, and no "thing," no event, no experience, nothing at all can ever drive a wedge between us and the God who loves us with the power of all creation and the plan to wrap up all of God's Story to bring about justice, peace, love, and eternal wisdom. In which story, to swipe words from C.S. Lewis' *The Last Battle*, "every chapter is better than the one before." Noticeably, Lewis called the story of the final kingdom "Chapter One of the Great Story which no one on earth has read" (*The Last Battle,* 211). Everything the characters of his seven volumes in *The Chronicles of Narnia* went through were but "the cover and the title page."

Positively Pauline.

Positively Romans 8.

The last word in the network of redemptive words is Victory, and each word in the network holds in its arms each of the other words so tightly the words become as inseparable as we are from God's love for us in Christ through the Spirit.

Questions for Reflection and Application

1. What does this hard look at Paul's sufferings do to your impression of him?

2. How can Paul still believe that "God's got this" after all he went through?

3. How do Paul's sufferings give him credibility to teach the Roman Christians about God and hope?

4. How can we be more than conquerors when we face difficulties?

5. Where in your life do you need Victory from God?

FOR FURTHER READING

C.S. Lewis, *The Last Battle* (New York: HarperCollins, 1998).

DIVINE FAITHFULNESS AND REDEMPTIVE PEACE

Romans 9:1–29

[1] I speak the truth in Christ—I am not lying, my conscience confirms it through the Holy Spirit—[2] I have great sorrow and unceasing anguish in my heart. [3] For I could wish that I myself were cursed and cut off from Christ for the sake of my people, those of my own race, [4] the people of Israel. Theirs is the adoption to sonship; theirs the divine glory, the covenants, the receiving of the law, the temple worship and the promises. [5] Theirs are the patriarchs, and from them is traced the human ancestry of the Messiah, who is God over all, forever praised! Amen.

[6] It is not as though God's word had failed. For not all who are descended from Israel are Israel. [7] Nor because they are his descendants are they all Abraham's children. On the contrary, "It is through Isaac that your offspring will be reckoned." [8] In other words, it is not the children by physical descent who are God's children, but it is the children of the promise who are regarded as Abraham's offspring. [9] For this was how the promise was stated: "At the appointed time I will return, and Sarah will have a son."

[10] Not only that, but Rebekah's children were conceived at the same time by our father Isaac. [11] Yet, before the twins were born or had done anything good or bad—in order that God's purpose in

election might stand: [12] *not by works but by him who calls—she was told, "The older will serve the younger."* [13] *Just as it is written: "Jacob I loved, but Esau I hated."*

[14] ***What then shall we say? Is God unjust?***

Not at all! [15] *For he says to Moses,*

"I will have mercy on whom I have mercy,

and I will have compassion on whom I have compassion."

[16] *It does not, therefore, depend on human desire or effort, but on God's mercy.* [17] *For Scripture says to Pharaoh: "I raised you up for this very purpose, that I might display my power in you and that my name might be proclaimed in all the earth."* [18] *Therefore God has mercy on whom he wants to have mercy, and he hardens whom he wants to harden.*

[19] ***One of you will say to me: "Then why does God still blame us?***

For who is able to resist his will?"

[Paul answers these questions with his own stinging, even accusing questions. I highlighted these to separate them from the imagined questions of those challenging Paul.]

[20] ***[1] But who are you, a human being, to talk back to God?***

[2] "Shall what is formed say to the one who formed it, 'Why did you make me like this?'"

[21] ***[3] Does not the potter have the right to make out of the same lump of clay some pottery for special purposes and some for common use?***

[22] ***[4] What if God, although choosing to show his wrath and make his power known, bore with great patience the objects of his wrath—prepared for destruction?***

[23] ***[5] What if he did this to make the riches of his glory known to the objects of his mercy, whom he prepared in advance for glory—*** [24] ***even us, whom he also called, not only from the Jews but also from the Gentiles?***

[25] *As he says in Hosea:*

"I will call them 'my people' who are not my people;
and I will call her 'my loved one' who is not my loved one,"
[26] *and,*
"In the very place where it was said to them,
'You are not my people,'
there they will be called 'children of the living God.' "
[27] *Isaiah cries out concerning Israel:*
"Though the number of the Israelites be like the sand by the sea,
only the remnant will be saved.

[28] *For the Lord will carry out*
his sentence on earth with speed and finality."
[29] *It is just as Isaiah said previously:*
"Unless the Lord Almighty
had left us descendants,
we would have become like Sodom,
we would have been like Gomorrah."

Many Bible readers consider Romans 9–11 the most difficult (to comprehend and to accept) section in the whole Bible. For many it flies in the face of so much of the rest of the Bible. Thus, one can ask after reading the three chapters, is every detail of every person's life plotted out by God in advance so much that an individual's eternal redemption was predetermined? (That view is called "meticulous providence.") Is Paul affirming that a death sentence of cancer for 20-year-old woman is God's actual doing? Romans 9–11 stumped me in my college days. I took a class on Romans with a wonderful Bible teacher, but we didn't make it past Romans 8! I asked the teacher what to read on 9–11, he recommended a book, I read it, and I was still stumped.

Over the years I have listened to many people attempt to explain this difficult set of three chapters. Gradually, and then almost suddenly, I came to the conclusion that there's a better way to look at it than through the lens of meticulous sovereignty and predestination as are taught in some forms of Calvinism. In my reflections on these three chapters perhaps this approach will help you as it has helped me.

Before we get there, though, a return to a theme I have mentioned many times. Romans 9–11 sums up Paul's responses to the questions of his critics. Today's passage begins by explaining *Israel's Story* in light of God's surprising expansion of Israel to include gentiles (without observance of the law). Romans 1–4 was more of a theological argument and Romans 9–11 is more of narrative or storied approach to his critics' questions. He learned each approach worked, or perhaps that one approach did and the other approach didn't, and these chapters become his own summary of how best to respond to those who question the ways of God. Think of his basic answer this way:

> God is faithful to his covenant with Abraham and Israel, in surprising ways, while also expanding Israel to include the gentiles, without law observance, and once again God is faithful, in surprising ways.

One More Time, Notice These Features

Questions burst from the pages again. They remind us of Romans 1–4's barrage of questions and answers. I have put the questions in bold face to make them more obvious, and I've highlighted his five questions back to his imagined challengers in bold italics (9:20–23). Not only do we notice the bursting forth of questions, but once again Paul goes totally biblical with another barrage of citations from Scripture.

This, too, looks just like Romans 1–4. So, it is reasonable to conclude the audience of Romans 1–4 and chapter 9 (through 11:12) is the same. Namely, here Paul is responding to questions he gets from his fellow Jews who either oppose his gospel or his fellow Jewish believers who think gentile believers need to observe the law of Moses. That group finds a personal representative in the Judge of 2:1, and this group is not the same as all Jews, all of Judaism, or even all Jewish believers. After all, Paul is a Jew. Romans 9:1–11:12 can be framed as inner Jewish discussions. A denominational debate. The gentiles can wait outside until they're done.

Privileges of God's People

One of the challenges Paul faced was so many (the vast majority actually) of his fellow Jews did not believe Jesus was Israel's Messiah and neither did they accept the gospel mission of the apostle Paul. This double rejection deeply troubled Paul, and he expresses his grief in Romans 9:2 after he has made it clear he's telling the utter truth: "I have great sorrow and unceasing anguish."

Why? Because, he says, "my people, those of my own race, the people of Israel," though they are God's chosen people for the blessing of the world (Genesis 12:3), they have not embraced Jesus of Nazareth, the one crucified and raised, as God's Messiah. Paul's heart is shredded over their unbelief, and he offers to be "cursed and cut off from Christ" for their redemption. This curse-me offer ascends from the waters of baptism (6:1–14) as he declares his willingness to go to the cross for his fellow Jews (9:3).

Israelites are the epicenter of God's redemptive work, and he mentions eight features of their dynamic privilege in God's plan (9:4–5). Here they are:

1. adoption to sonship
2. the divine glory
3. the covenants
4. receiving of the law,
5. temple worship
6. the promises
7. the patriarchs
8. the human ancestry of the Messiah.

None of this has been undone; God is true to his promises and covenant with Israel (11:29), even if it is (as we are about to see) full of surprises and wrinkles in the unfolding of that plan. Most of these eight items are immediately clear, but #2 and #8 need a little explanation.

To begin with, the NIV added the word "divine" to "glory" and it is not certain that "divine" should be added. Glory is mentioned a number of times in Romans where it refers to the final glorification of humans, of those made in God's image (cf. 8:17–18, 21, 30). Yes, but it also does refer to God's own splendor and glory (5:2; 15:6–9). The context of the above list matters, and the list is about Israel, God's people, and Paul's fellow Jews. Glory is listed between adoption and covenant. Since sonship is about *Israel's* adoption to be placed in God's covenant family (Genesis 12; Exodus 19–24), the word "glory" most likely evokes the presence of God's glory with *Israel* in its time of wandering (Exodus 16:7, 10; 40:34–35). Richard Longenecker, who studied and taught and wrote about Romans for four decades before writing up his commentary, goes so far as to say "all Jewish and Christian hearers" would know that this reference to the splendor and glory would be about God's special presence "among his people" Israel (*Romans*, 784).

The second item in need of explanation is #8. Paul adds "who is God over all, forever praised" (9:5). Paul cracks open a divine mystery, one that was tested in the church in the third and fourth centuries, when he precedes "God over all" with Jesus. That is, *Jesus is God over all.* One can add to this verse John 1:1; 20:28; and Titus 2:13. These verses clearly affirm that Jesus of Nazareth, the human being, was God and thus the God-man.

Surprises for God's people

To travel along the bumpy, twisty, and thoroughly surprising path from verse 6 to 29 in Romans 9 we need to ponder what challenges Paul is meeting from those who are asking him so many, many questions. Paul does not drive a hard theology here so much as press his critics to realize but one great big idea:

> God's choice to include gentiles in the people of God fits into God's surprising ways in the history of Israel.

What surprised them the most, no doubt, is that gentiles were included in this most privileged history of Israel *without having to observe the law of Moses.* For some of the Powerless, especially for the Judge, non-observance of the law for those in the people of God just doesn't make sense. One can hear them muttering *chapter and verse, please.* Paul makes sense of gentile inclusion without law observance by appealing to Israel's God as the God of great surprises.

Some critics think the unbelief (in Jesus as Messiah) of so many Jews *questions the veracity of God's promises, that is, of "God's word"* because "not all who are descendants from Israel are Israel" (9:6). Paul clarifies. In the outworking of the divine plan there is more to the redemptive plan than physical heritage: not all have been "Abraham's children"

(9:7). He said this to the Judge at 2:28–29. This is the heart of everything in the rest of today's passage. Being born in Israel does not absolutely guarantee inclusion in God's plan of redemption. He makes this point with Isaac (not Ishmael) and with Jacob (not Esau). God surprised the parents of both of these boys (9:7–13). Michael Gorman says it this way: Paul has learned that "God acts freely, faithfully, and mercifully" (Gorman, *Romans*, 221).

Some question *God's fairness or justice* (9:14) and actually suggest God is capricious. Paul answers with a quotation from Exodus 33:19 that God is the One who elects on the basis of mercy (9:15–18). That question is stacked next to a similar question (9:19). The question haunts Bible readers: How can God judge, and thus "blame" those guilty of disobedience and unbelief if God is the one who determines in advance who does what? Paul lights this one up with strong reactive questions. Five of them. Notice them in the translation above in italics. With echoes of Job 38–42's powerful indictment of human arrogance in the face of divine inscrutability, Paul simply undresses the challenge by arguing that God is God and infinite and omniscient, and humans are not God, are finite, and don't know all that much. God is good, God is loving, and yet God can do what God wants to do.

Third, Paul explores *two hypotheticals*. What *IF* God wanted to split humans into two camps? What *IF* God did all this so God could get all things ready for the expansion of the gospel to the gentiles? (9:22–24). It reads as if Paul knows that he does not know the mind of God. So he merely offers two possibilities, two totally hypothetical answers of why God may be doing what God is doing. I agree with Gorman: this is not a "doctrine of double predestination" but "the freedom of God to surprise people with mercy" (Gorman, *Romans*, 223).

However, it is not clear that Paul actually answers those possibilities. Instead, he moves on with a powerful collusion of Bible verses that all support God's very merciful, surprising ways.

We don't know why God does what God does,
but what we know is what God does:
God surprises.

The biggest surprise for many of his listeners was that just being born a Jew does not mean one is part of the divine redemptive plan through Israel. The Bible shows what he means so Paul launches into Bible verse memory time. He quotes from Hosea 2, then backs up to Hosea 1, then he turns to the prophet of prophets, Isaiah, starting with Isaiah 10 and then back to Isaiah 1. The impact of these verses is pointed: *God's choice of who is next in line in the people of God has always been surprising.* Those "not my people" can be added to "my people" and become "children of the living God" or the "remnant" (9:25–29).

Therefore, the gentiles who believe in Jesus, the Messiah, God incarnate, are every bit a part of Israel.

Questions for Reflection and Application

1. What do you think of the idea that the audience for chapters 9–11 is the same as Paul's intended audience for chapters 1–4, that this is an inner Jewish discussion?

2. What caused Paul sorrow and anguish?

3. What privileges do the Israelites hold in God's covenant?

4. Have you ever been taught the meticulous sovereignty view of Romans 9–11? How does this explanation compare to that in your mind?

5. How does God's work surprise you as you read this passage?

HUMAN FAITHFULNESS AND REDEMPTIVE PEACE

Romans 9:30–10:21

[30] ***What then shall we say?***

That the Gentiles, who did not pursue righteousness, have obtained it, a righteousness that is by faith; [31] *but the people of Israel, who pursued the law as the way of righteousness, have not attained their goal.*

[32] ***Why not?***

Because they pursued it not by faith but as if it were by works. They stumbled over the stumbling stone. [33] *As it is written:*

"See, I lay in Zion a stone that causes people to stumble
and a rock that makes them fall,
and the one who believes in him will never be put to shame."

[10:1] *Brothers and sisters, my heart's desire and prayer to God for the Israelites is that they may be saved.* [2] *For I can testify about them that they are zealous for God, but their zeal is not based on knowledge.* [3] *Since they did not know the righteousness of God and sought to establish their own, they did not submit to God's righteousness.* [4] *Christ is the culmination of the law so that there may be righteousness for everyone who believes.*

[5] Moses writes this about the righteousness that is by the law: "The person who does these things will live by them." [6] But the righteousness that is by faith says: "Do not say in your heart, 'Who will ascend into heaven?' " (that is, to bring Christ down) [7] "or 'Who will descend into the deep?' " (that is, to bring Christ up from the dead). [8] But what does it say? "The word is near you; it is in your mouth and in your heart," that is, the message concerning faith that we proclaim: [9] If you declare with your mouth, "Jesus is Lord," and believe in your heart that God raised him from the dead, you will be saved. [10] For it is with your heart that you believe and are justified, and it is with your mouth that you profess your faith and are saved. [11] As Scripture says, "Anyone who believes in him will never be put to shame." [12] For there is no difference between Jew and Gentile—the same Lord is Lord of all and richly blesses all who call on him, [13] for, "Everyone who calls on the name of the Lord will be saved."

[14] How, then, can they call on the one they have not believed in? And how can they believe in the one of whom they have not heard? And how can they hear without someone preaching to them? [15] And how can anyone preach unless they are sent? As it is written: "How beautiful are the feet of those who bring good news!"

[16] But not all the Israelites accepted the good news. For Isaiah says, "Lord, who has believed our message?" [17] Consequently, faith comes from hearing the message, and the message is heard through the word about Christ. [18] But I ask: Did they not hear? Of course they did:

> *"Their voice has gone out into all the earth,*
> *their words to the ends of the world."*
>
> *[19] Again I ask: Did Israel not understand? First, Moses says,*
>
> *"I will make you envious by those who are not a nation;*
> *I will make you angry by a nation that has no understanding."*

> [20] *And Isaiah boldly says,*
> *"I was found by those who did not seek me;*
> *I revealed myself to those who did not ask for me."*
> [21] *But concerning Israel he says,*
> *"All day long I have held out my hands*
> *to a disobedient and obstinate people."*

There are two temperature systems in the world. Every time Kris and I travel either to Turkey and Greece to see sites of the apostle Paul or to Israel to see sites of Jesus, we struggle to know the temperature. Is it Celsius or Fahrenheit? Telling us it is above 30 (Celsius) does not register that it may be above 90 (Fahrenheit). For us, one works, and one doesn't. What may not be known to many readers of this study guide is that when Kris and I were grade schoolers we experienced a push from the USA's education brass to convert the country to the metric and to the Celsius system. That conversion did not happen. So we struggle and, when in Turkey, we have to ask a tour guide what the equivalent temperature is in Fahrenheit. The tour guide always knows. Our system does not work in Turkey. (By the way, it's a beautiful country.)

The Christ System Vs. the Law System

Like the Celsius and the Fahrenheit systems, there are, theoretically at least, two systems for achieving righteousness. With the gentiles still very much on his mind, Paul says the gentiles are known in the Jewish world as not pursuing righteousness but they have found "a righteousness that is by faith" (9:30). The "people of Israel," have chosen a different system, one shaped by pursuing the law "by works" (9:31–32). Here's the problem. One works, and one does not; one reaches the "goal" and one does not.

What Paul says next entirely reshapes what many readers expect him to say, and he doesn't. He doesn't say they became sinners and that leads to Agent Sin and Death because they remain in the Adam line. He does not say that, though he implies it. What he does say is that the people of Israel tripped over a tripping stone. The tripping stone is a "stone" and a "rock" and a person, and the person is Jesus. In other words, the problem with the law system is that it is the Adam line and not the Christ line, and one person participates in the Christ line—as Paul is about to say—by faith, not by the works of the law (see pp. 187–189). The two systems then are not just faith and works. They are:

Adam	Christ
Law and Moses	Spirit
Works	Faith
Law righteousness	Faith righteousness

Always keep this chart in mind when Paul talks about the importance of faith. The *most important* word is "Christ"—the Christ system is the system that leads to righteousness. The problem with the Adam system, then, is that it is not the Christ system.

The Christ System: He Is the Law's Culmination

God's plan in history was to reveal his Son as the Agent of righteousness. When the computer arrived, typewriters moved into the slower lane. When a bicycle with hand adjusted gears arrived, the single gear bicycle took a loss. When espresso coffee machines showed up in the USA, drip coffee got put where it belongs (enough said). When Christ arrived, the Adam and Law and Works system became the preliminary indicators of what would be found in its fullness in Christ. So, to Romans 10:4 we go first: "Christ is the *culmination* of the law." What the law wanted to be and what it was designed to be was not to be realized until Christ, who is the goal, the telos, the fulfillment of the law. Saying Christ is the culmination does not erase the law. Christ reveals that the law is the "first" revelation and he is the "final" revelation. The Christ system, because it is not the Moses-law-works system, produces righteousness "for everyone who believes." And that means not by works and not by the law and not by Moses.

The crucial moment is the advent of Christ. Everything hinges on recognizing who Jesus is and the redemption he alone brings. Because of who Christ is and what he has done, Paul emotes *for* his fellow Israelites "that they may be saved" (10:1) and *about* them because their zeal is misplaced (10:2) and misdirected toward themselves (10:3). Prior to Christ, Paul was like them; after encountering Christ on the Damascus Road (Acts 9), Paul saw his past in completely different terms.

The Christ System: By Faith

The rest of Romans 10 flows directly out of the above lists and Romans 10:4's claim that *there is but one way to true righteousness and that way is by faith in Christ.* The previous passage emphasized divine faithfulness with abundant surprises, and today's passage emphasizes the necessity of human faithfulness to participate in those abundant surprises. Our hands once again need to get a good grip on what Paul means by faith. The word moves across a spectrum from an initial moment of trust (believing) to a life of trusting (allegiance, faithfulness) to what a person believes (the faith). Some apparently believe and then fade away. Genuine faith in the Bible is a faith that perseveres, that is, true faith is allegiance and faithfulness.

Paul, in a move so clever many still struggle to figure out just what he's saying in 10:6–8, claims righteousness by faith was taught by Moses. I think it is best to read 10:6's and 10:7's questions as questions by the Weak or by the Judge, and the parentheses as Paul's own response. Plus, Paul seems to have another character (or it's himself) uttering words in 10:6, and that imagined character on the stage is Mr. Righteousness himself, who says "Do not say in your heart" (10:6) and then at the end says, "The word is near you . . . in your mouth . . . in your heart" (10:8). As I say, it's clever. I reformat this approach to help it make sense:

> [Mr. Righteousness:] [6] But the righteousness that is by faith says [quoting the Weak:] "Do not say in your heart, 'Who will ascend into heaven?' "([Paul's comment:] that is, to bring Christ down) [7] "or [quoting the Weak:] 'Who will descend into the deep?'" ([Paul's comment:] that is, to bring Christ up from the dead).
>
> [Mr. Righteousness:] [8] But what does it say? "The word is near you; it is in your mouth and in your heart," that is, the message concerning faith that we proclaim . . .

He quotes words from Deuteronomy 30:12–14 (about covenant renewal, starting in the heart) to illustrate what "righteousness by faith" is, where the emphasis is found in Romans 10:8's that true faith is "in your mouth" and "in your heart." He interprets those as confessing with the mouth that "Jesus is Lord" and believing in the heart "that God raised him from the dead" (10:9), and confession-shaped faith leads to being right with God and being saved (10:10). Again, this all leads to why gentiles are now part of the people of God, the expanded Israel: anyone who believes in Christ is in (10:11–13).

The heart's cry of both 9:2–3 and 10:1 is that his fellow Israelites would recognize who Jesus is and offer their allegiance to him. That can only happen if preachers preach to them, and there will not be enough preachers unless some are sent (10:14–15). Please read 10:13–15 carefully and notice how one crucial word gets repeated as a chain of links forms. The words are calls, believe, hear, preach, sent. (The word "sent" is repeated in the assumption in 10:16's "Who has believed *our* [the ones sent] message?")

At the heart of his heart's cry is awareness that his fellow Israelites over time have not responded in faithfulness to the message of God sent to them through the prophets Isaiah and Moses and back to Isaiah for two more verses (all in Romans 10:16–21). Each of these Bible verses reveals that Israel has heard God's message but *not all believed*. Which reminds us that not all Israel is Israel (9:6), and that some who do believe are gentiles. He quotes Isaiah to remind the Weak of God's faithful and often surprising ways: "I was found by those who did not seek me; I revealed myself to those who did not ask for me" (Isaiah 65:1 quoted at Romans 10:20).

But, as chapter eleven quickly observes, God has not rejected Israel!

Paul's message in Romans 9 and 10 reveals the relentless faithfulness of God to Israel, Paul's own relentless love for Israel, his belief that Israel's own Scriptures establishes that Jesus is the Messiah for them, and his relentless plea for the gospel to be offered to them by as many as possible. Those who respond with faith in Christ discover redemption.

Questions for Reflection and Application

1. What are the problems with the Adam system?

2. How does Christ function as the culmination of the law?

3. What is included in the spectrum of what Paul means by "faith"?

4. What does it mean that "not all Israel is Israel," and why does this grieve Paul?

5. How do you feel toward people who have heard the story of Jesus yet do not believe in him?

THE REMNANT IN GOD'S REDEMPTIVE PEACE

Romans 11:1–12

[1] ***I ask then: Did God reject his people?***

By no means! I am an Israelite myself, a descendant of Abraham, from the tribe of Benjamin. [2] *God did not reject his people, whom he foreknew. Don't you know what Scripture says in the passage about Elijah—how he appealed to God against Israel:* [3] *"Lord, they have killed your prophets and torn down your altars; I am the only one left, and they are trying to kill me"?* [4] *And what was God's answer to him? "I have reserved for myself seven thousand who have not bowed the knee to Baal."* [5] *So too, at the present time there is a remnant chosen by grace.* [6] *And if by grace, then it cannot be based on works; if it were, grace would no longer be grace.*

[7] ***What then?***

What the people of Israel sought so earnestly they did not obtain. The elect among them did, but the others were hardened, [8] *as it is written:*

> *"God gave them a spirit of stupor,*
> *eyes that could not see*

and ears that could not hear,
to this very day."
[9] *And David says:*
"May their table become a snare and a trap,
a stumbling block and a retribution for them.
[10] *May their eyes be darkened so they cannot see,*
and their backs be bent forever."

[11] *Again I ask: Did they stumble so as to fall beyond recovery?*

Not at all! Rather, because of their transgression, salvation has come to the Gentiles to make Israel envious. [12] *But if their transgression means riches for the world, and their loss means riches for the Gentiles, how much greater riches will their full inclusion bring!*

Three questions with three answers finish off Paul's attempt to convince his readers/listeners of God's faithfulness to the covenant with Abraham and Israel in spite of God's very surprising ways. The inclusion of gentiles into the people of God never offended Jewish sensibilities. Not only does the Old Testament include examples of gentile faith in the God of Israel, but by the time of Paul Judaism had formed into the kind of "religion" that made "conversion" possible. The process included, most likely, a kind of ceremonial entrance that included commitment to the laws of Moses, an initial sacrifice in the temple, and proselyte baptism. The lack of evidence for exactly what was required blurs our confidence, but one can be assured circumcision and an initial sacrifice in Jerusalem were involved.

Paul's approach, however, surprised Jewish sensibilities. He "admitted" gentiles into the people of God *without requiring a commitment to the God-given laws of Moses*. The sole requirement was faith embodied in baptism into Christ. Anything more than faith Paul called "works of the law," and we know he couldn't stop talking about grace alone and faith alone. Since observance of the law gave Israel a public identity, and since Paul taught gentiles not to observe the law, the first question above (11:1) becomes a knee-jerk common question Paul was asked. His second question allows him to extend his answer to the first question, but his third question leads to a fresh explanation of God's plans.

Is the God of Israel Rejecting Israel?

Paul lands gently on the edge of a balance beam in Romans 11:1–6. The question is, Has God shoved off the stage his own people, Israel? The answer is "By no means!" and the exclamation point in English translations interprets the answer as something Phoebe said firmly, if not with a raise in decibels. Landing on the edge of the balance beam will mean some listeners of this letter will not be entirely convinced.

Paul defends his landing with a six-fold response. God has not rejected his people because:

1. Paul himself has solid Jewish credentials (Israelite, from Abraham, from Benjamin) and he believes (11:1). Therefore, Israel has not been rejected.
2. God has never and never will reject foreknown Israel (11:2).[1] Therefore, Israel has not been rejected.
3. Elijah learned that though he thought he was the only faithful person left that God still had "seven thousand" faithful (11:2–4).
4. God's plan has always involved a faithful "remnant" that are faithful "by grace" (11:5). Notice 9:25–27. Therefore, Israel has not been rejected.

5. God's plan works out for those whom he has selected (or elected) (11:7). Therefore, Israel has not been rejected.
6. God's plan involves a hardening of the unfaithful (11:7–9). Therefore, Israel has not been rejected.

The problem with his landing will be said by his critics with force: *well, then, Paul, has not God rejected all but the remnant?* Paul thinks he has stuck his landing by appealing to the always-surprising ways of God in the past. Those ways involved Israel as made up of both the faithful and the unfaithful. We are back to an early line in chapter nine when he said, "For not all who are descended from Israel are Israel" (9:6). Birth in Israel does not make a person a faithful Israelite. Nor does circumcision, observance of Sabbath, or commitment to food laws make a person a faithful Israelite. God's faithfulness does not require everyone in Israel being faithful.

Faithfulness flows from God's grace and God's election (11:7) of those whom he calls the ones "he foreknew" (11:2). The Bible's theology, to adapt our image, lands firmly on the balance beam, and that dead-center of the beam landing is on two feet: first, God's gracious election of people and, second, the people's heart-based commitments and allegiance to God. If we glory in a one-footed landing, we fail the Bible's own balance. The first foot to land is God's, the second one belongs to the ones responding in faithful allegiance.

A one-footed landing neglects the necessity of the proper human response. A kind of "just preach grace" or "just teach election" and the elect will eventually burst from their shells. Those who refuse, for such a view, are those whom God "hardens." One can put it this way: routine, constant rejection of the ways of God make a person dull and eventually incapable of responding to God's ways (11:8–10). At times the Bible appeals to divine providence for human rejection of God, but most of the time the Bible accuses humans of turning from God, not God from humans.

A proper balance prevents elitism. Yes, not all believe; yes, some do. That does not make believers the elite of this world with unbelievers as the inferior dullards. If we think again of the Powerless and the Powerful, we recall the stereotyping by one or the other. That can happen whenever one appeals to the idea of the remnant. The remnant are not in the people of God because they deserve it; they are the products of God's own grace. If they become conceited in themselves, they, too, can be lopped off (see 11:18–21). In many ways America's evangelicals are described accurately as those who think of themselves as the elite among God's people. And some groups within evangelicalism think they are the elite of the elite. Arrogance about one's (presumed) high status among the people of God flies in the face of every line in Romans 9–11. May God have mercy.

In fact, God's mercy explodes in Romans 11 because the remnant anticipates an abundant and flourishing fullness in the future. As Thomas Hoyt once wrote, "The preservation of a part—the remnant—gives promissory assurance for the future of the whole" (Hoyt, "Romans," 266). His hopeful approach to the idea of remnant beautifully anticipates what Paul is about to say in our next small paragraph and then in the rest of chapter eleven.

The Surprising Seventh Explanation

Paul's previously-listed six explanations for the fact that some in Israel do not believe Jesus is God's Messiah now meets a surprising explanation, an explanation set up with a new question: "Did they stumble so as to fall beyond recovery?"

In fact, the rejecters have not fully rejected God. They have only "stumbled" and are not "beyond recovery" (11:11). Did they stumble beyond recovery? Paul's answer, again said with full force by Phoebe, is "Not at all!"

There's hope for recovery because Israel's stumbling stands in the record as a "transgression" that both (1) makes "salvation" available to gentiles and, at the very same time, (2) provokes Israel's envy that will lead to their recovery (11:11). Paul marches farther into the future: Israel's future recovery will bring about a "fullness" to the people of God—both Jews and gentiles worshiping God (11:12). Paul's point is that Israel's rejection leads to gentile acceptance in the now and Israel's acceptance in the future, forming a fullness to the people of God.

So, God has not rejected Israel. God has a surprising plan for including gentiles so God can eventually break through to Israel.

Questions for Reflection and Application

1. If gentile inclusion itself into God's people wasn't offensive to Jews of Paul's time, why were the Weak/Powerless in Rome so offended by Paul's message?

2. What are the details of Paul's response to the question of whether God was rejecting or abandoning Israel? Do you think the listeners were convinced?

3. How do God and people make up the two-footed landing in the balance beam analogy?

4. How does Paul find hope for the salvation of both gentiles and Jews in the face of Israel's rejection of Jesus as Messiah?

5. When have you experienced feeling like one of the "elite" in faith? Or, when have you felt left out by other people who considered themselves "elite"?

THE GENTILES IN GOD'S REDEMPTIVE PEACE

Romans 11:13–24

[13] I am talking to you Gentiles. Inasmuch as I am the apostle to the Gentiles, I take pride in my ministry [14] in the hope that I may somehow arouse my own people to envy and save some of them. [15] For if their rejection brought reconciliation to the world, what will their acceptance be but life from the dead? [16] If the part of the dough offered as firstfruits is holy, then the whole batch is holy; if the root is holy, so are the branches.

[17] If some of the branches have been broken off, and you, though a wild olive shoot, have been grafted in among the others and now share in the nourishing sap from the olive root, [18] do not consider yourself to be superior to those other branches. If you do, consider this: You do not support the root, but the root supports you. [19] You will say then, "Branches were broken off so that I could be grafted in." [20] Granted. But they were broken off because of unbelief, and you stand by faith. Do not be arrogant, but tremble. [21] For if God did not spare the natural branches, he will not spare you either.

[22] Consider therefore the kindness and sternness of God: sternness to those who fell, but kindness to you, provided that you

continue in his kindness. Otherwise, you also will be cut off. [23] *And if they do not persist in unbelief, they will be grafted in, for God is able to graft them in again.* [24] *After all, if you were cut out of an olive tree that is wild by nature, and contrary to nature were grafted into a cultivated olive tree, how much more readily will these, the natural branches, be grafted into their own olive tree!*

Elitism and stereotyping of others sprout in most churches. Sometimes it begins with one person and then spreads into a small group, and at times a small group becomes a collection of small groups, and before long we watch a movement in action. Such sprouts pop into visibility out of traditional church because traditional churches tend to resist new ideas. Once these sprouts, or dissidents, pop out, they inevitably begin to look down on the traditional church. They begin to speak in what is sometimes called an anti-rhetoric. That is, the dissidents define themselves over against their former fellowship and think just about everything the traditionalists do is wrong. The rhetoric becomes dichotomous. A group think grows and before long they become the superior group.

Paul knows about something similar happening in Rome: the Powerful (gentile) believers convinced themselves that they were the best form of the Christian faith in Rome. They were living in gospel freedom while the Powerless were tied to the laws of Moses. It wasn't that simple, of course, but group think doesn't budge from simplicities and inaccuracies about the Other. The Powerful exploit their platform to narrate the official story that excludes the Other, they attempt to gaslight the vulnerable, they elevate the loyal insiders, they exclude and silence the Other, and they pretend to live in a world in which only the Powerful matter.

Today's passage points a long finger at the Powerful in Rome with a piercing warning. Which is why Paul begins with "I am talking to you Gentiles" (11:13). Phoebe, in reading this letter aloud to the various house churches, surely looked directly at the gentile believers in the room. And spoke to them until she got to the end of (our) chapter eleven, though you might wonder if she turned to the entire room when she got to verse twenty-five. I think she kept her eyes glued to the Powerful all the way through verse thirty-six.

The big message of 11:13–36 is, If God can surprise many in the history of Israel, he can surprise the gentile believers too. So, they are to walk in faithfulness or they, too, may discover the severity of God's discipline.

Gentile Faith Leads to Israelite Faith

There is a development in God's plan. In verse eleven Paul saw Israel's disobedience promoting gentile obedience to the plan of God, and in verse twelve the inclusion of gentiles would lead to the fullness of the people of God. Verses thirteen through sixteen explain what can be called "gospel envy." The arising of gentile faith in the God of Israel and his Messiah arouses envy and repentance among Jews. Paul then uses two images: dough in a batch, roots and branches. The dough and roots refer to the remnant, and the batch and branches to the fullness of the people of God. The fullness is the inclusion of gentile believers along with the messianic remnant (11:16).

Remember this: Paul pounds the pulpit on a future awakening of Israel to faith in Jesus as God's Messiah. His mission to the gentiles will provoke Jews to reconsider their covenant relation to God.

Gentile Faith Must Be Faithful

Root and branches now get explained. Gentiles, who are but "wild olive shoot[s]," have been grafted into the root stock of the Israelite tree. That is, they are now part of God's covenant and promises to Abraham and to Israel. But this does not make them "superior to those other branches" (11:18). Just how they got that sensibility is not clear. What is clear is that the Roman way was one of status climbing and honor. Some of these gentile believers transferred their Roman ways into the church, and Paul will have none of it. Gentiles need the root stock, rather than the root stock needing them.

Paul says the unbelievers have been snipped off the root stock–the covenant people–because of "unbelief" (11:19–20). The gentiles believe, but he says to them "Do not be arrogant," which can be translated "don't think high-status thoughts." Instead, they are to stand in awe before God because the God who snipped off previous branches can do the same with the gentile wild olive shoots. There can be a "sternness of God" that can lead to their being "cut off" (11:22). In their awe before God, they need to ponder God's "kindness."

In fact, God can graft previously unbelieving Jews back into the tree. It is so important here to see that Paul does not see the church replacing Israel as the people of God. The church instead is the expansion of Israel to include believing gentiles. Of course, only those who believe are in that people of God, but it is the same old people of God—the Israel of faith (9:6).

In this passage we are back again with the stereotyping by the Powerful of the Powerless. The Powerful are despising the Powerless for their "weakness" of needing the law while the Powerful are claiming superiority because they have been grafted in to the root stock and are now living in that tradition of Israel in freedom from the law. Attitudes like those of the Powerful diminish the expansive work of God and destroy the unity of the fellowship. The solution, as it has been from the outset of this guide, is to welcome one another as siblings in Christ by learning to live in the way of Christ. As Sarah

Lancaster says it, "Competition among the members of the church is completely ruled out" (Lancaster, *Romans,* 192).

And what does this mean for us? We, too, just like Israel and just like Paul's gentile audience, must be faithful to enter into the kingdom of God. Faithfulness is not sinlessness, but a life of ongoing trust, of obedience to the will of God, of respect for the surprising ways of God, of confidence in the plan of God with Israel who has only temporarily fallen away, and it is at the same time a profound reverence and awe before God who, after all, can be surprisingly stern.

May God not need to be stern with us!

Questions for Reflection and Application

1. What are the Strong/Powerful gentile believers in Rome doing wrong?

2. Underline the "you" and "they/their/Israel" language in today's passage. What does this tell you about the intended audience for these verses?

3. What does "gospel envy" mean?

4. Go find online a video about grafting olive branches. What understanding does that visual add to your grasp of this passage?

5. What are some ways you can change your language to carefully avoid any claims that the church replaces Israel as the people of God? How can you explain it instead?

THE MYSTERY OF GOD'S REDEMPTIVE PEACE

Romans 11:25–36

[25] I do not want you to be ignorant of this mystery, brothers and sisters, so that you may not be conceited: Israel has experienced a hardening in part until the full number of the Gentiles has come in, [26] and in this way all Israel will be saved. As it is written:

> *"The deliverer will come from Zion;*
> *he will turn godlessness away from Jacob.*
> *[27] And this is my covenant with them*
> *when I take away their sins."*

[28] As far as the gospel is concerned, they are enemies for your sake; but as far as election is concerned, they are loved on account of the patriarchs, [29] for God's gifts and his call are irrevocable. [30] Just as you who were at one time disobedient to God have now received mercy as a result of their disobedience, [31] so they too have now become disobedient in order that they too may now receive mercy as a result of God's mercy to you. [32] For God has bound everyone over to disobedience so that he may have mercy on them all.

[33] Oh, the depth of the riches of the wisdom and knowledge of God!
How unsearchable his judgments,
and his paths beyond tracing out!
[34] "Who has known the mind of the Lord?
Or who has been his counselor?"
[35] "Who has ever given to God,
that God should repay them?"
[36] For from him and through him and for him are all things.
To him be the glory forever! Amen.

Today's passage explains the mystery of the divine plan with Israel and the gentiles. Paradoxically, for Paul a "mystery" is something now known by revelation that was previously unknown. This divine mystery now disclosed taps in our passage on a rare chord in Paul: the eventual salvation of "all" (more below). The mystery then also means the Powerful and the Powerless ought to see themselves as siblings in God's family, to cease their stereotyping of the others, and to fellowship with one another. But Paul being Paul, he has to get into the weeds, and at times the weeds itch our skin.

Let me back off the intensity of the first century Jew-gentile tension. What Paul says in all of Romans 9–11 speaks from our pulpits in a strong voice that we will not solidify unity with one another until we see one another as co-participants in God's saving plan. That does not mean we will always agree or find a consensus. In fact, disagreement comes with the territory of passion for God's mission in this world. If we can learn to view our disagreements from the end when both sides will be conformed to Christ in the kingdom of God, we will improve our communications—in the very midst of our disagreements. Some disagreements are worth the battle. Not always. The Powerless and the Powerful both thought their battle was worth it, and Paul inserted himself right in the middle—with Phoebe reading his letter—to let them know they were fighting in the wrong battle.

Hardening and Disobedience Are Not Permanent

Paul's instructions to the Powerful continue by referring to their arrogance again in 11:25 (cf. 11:18, 20). Two terms explain the mystery of including gentiles while snipping off unbelieving covenant people: a divine hardness and disobedience (11:25, 31). The Godward explanation, hardening, and the human-ward explanation, disobedience, mesh together with bright lights forcing their way through a dark tunnel. The Godward hardening lasts only "until the full number of the Gentiles has come in" (11:25), which means the hardening is temporary and has a purpose: so that space can be given for gentiles to hear the gospel and respond to Jesus. Once again, God proves faithful, and God does not reject Israel.

As in the previous passage so here: we need the balance. If we focus too much on hardening, we can make God morally questionable—how can God hold someone accountable in judgment for something he "made" them do? If we focus too much on the human side, on disobedience, we contend humans can do what they cannot do on their own. Humans are in need of God's love, God's grace, and God's intervention. In some way both hardening and disobedience describe the very same reality of a person's or, as here, an ethnic group's salvation. That is, Jews and gentiles.

The Mystery's Final Aim

The weeds of this passage lead to some itching. The final aim is what itches many readers: "all Israel will be saved" (11:26).

Does "all" really mean "in every single Israelite/Jew who has lived, is living, and will live"? That question could have been asked back at 11:12 when Paul spoke of their "full inclusion." Plus, even more is said about what "all" might mean. Our question swells at 11:32 when Paul says, "For God has enclosed all in unpersuasion so he may show compassion on all" (my translation). The "all" with "Israel" is one ethnic group; the two uses of "all" in verse thirty-two, however, seems to indicate *every human being ever.* There are only two possibilities here. Either Paul means every human being will be finally saved or his "all" does not mean every human being. In which case, it means "all (believers)." Paul's constant theme of "by faith" establishes the probability that his "all" here means believers, among both Jews and gentiles. Notice 11:14 spoke of saving "some," which recalled his theme about the "remnant" (9:27), and he also spoke of "acceptance" by faith in 11:15, 20, 22, 23. And notice too that those saved will be saved by the "deliverer" who proceeds from Zion (11:26[1]), that is, by Christ alone. Paul does not think salvation is possible apart from believing.

Paul's heart is for his people (9:1–5; 10:1–4). They participate in God's "election" because they are "loved" by God (11:28) and will experience a full inclusion and acceptance because of God's compassion and mercy (11:31). God remains faithful to his promises to Abraham because "God's gifts and his call are *irrevocable*" (11:29, my emphasis). In some sense Israel remains, and again we appeal to 9:6's flashpoint: "For not all who are descended from Israel are Israel." Israel for Paul refers to the obedient, faithful, Messiah-trusting Israelites. Which for Paul seems also to include gentile believers in the Jewish Messiah.

God is generous and that's enough for me.

C'mon, people, let's give God a big shout.

One can easily get caught up with Paul in the glory of God's mysterious redemption plan of working here with

Israel and there with gentiles and then again with Israel—all the while remaining faithful to the Abrahamic covenant! Paul seems to have peered over the edge of time and glimpsed the glory of the future, and it leads him to exult in the "riches of the wisdom and knowledge of God" as well as in the inscrutable ways of God. Like Job, he knows he's come to the end of human comprehension. He throws his arms up and drops all his arguments, and stands amazed before the omniscient, good God.

He gives God a big shout: "To him be the glory forever!" (11:33–36).

Any reading of Romans 9–11 that ends up not giving God glory for his surprising generosity and goodness, all rooted in God's expansive mercy and love, fails to read the text well.

Where Paul ends, we are to end too. Let us sing the doxology.

Questions for Reflection and Application

1. What does it mean for God to "harden" people?

2. What role do humans and their will play in their choices to obey or disobey God?

3. Who is included in the "all" who will be saved?

4. How does Paul turn all this discussion toward glorifying God?

5. How have you dealt with serious disagreements with fellow believers in the past? What would you like to do differently in the future based on what you have gained from this study?

THE EMBODIED LIFE OF REDEMPTIVE PEACE

Romans 12:1–21

[1] Therefore, I urge you, brothers and sisters, in view of God's mercy, to offer your bodies as a living sacrifice, holy and pleasing to God—this is your true and proper worship. [2] Do not conform to the pattern of this world, but be transformed by the renewing of your mind. Then you will be able to test and approve what God's will is—his good, pleasing and perfect will.

[3] For by the grace given me I say to every one of you: Do not think of yourself more highly than you ought, but rather think of yourself with sober judgment, in accordance with the faith God has distributed to each of you. [4] For just as each of us has one body with many members, and these members do not all have the same function, [5] so in Christ we, though many, form one body, and each member belongs to all the others. [6] We have different gifts, according to the grace given to each of us. If your gift is prophesying, then prophesy in accordance with your faith; [7] if it is serving, then serve; if it is teaching, then teach; [8] if it is to encourage, then give encouragement; if it is giving, then give generously; if it is to lead, do it diligently; if it is to show mercy, do it cheerfully.

[9] *Love must be sincere. Hate what is evil; cling to what is good.* [10] *Be devoted to one another in love. Honor one another above yourselves.* [11] *Never be lacking in zeal, but keep your spiritual fervor, serving the Lord.* [12] *Be joyful in hope, patient in affliction, faithful in prayer.* [13] *Share with the Lord's people who are in need. Practice hospitality.*

[14] *Bless those who persecute you; bless and do not curse.* [15] *Rejoice with those who rejoice; mourn with those who mourn.* [16] *Live in harmony with one another. Do not be proud, but be willing to associate with people of low position. Do not be conceited.*

[17] *Do not repay anyone evil for evil. Be careful to do what is right in the eyes of everyone.* [18] *If it is possible, as far as it depends on you, live at peace with everyone.* [19] *Do not take revenge, my dear friends, but leave room for God's wrath, for it is written: "It is mine to avenge; I will repay," says the Lord.* [20] *On the contrary:*

> *"If your enemy is hungry, feed him;*
> *if he is thirsty, give him something to drink.*
> *In doing this, you will heap burning coals on his head."*

[21] *Do not be overcome by evil, but overcome evil with good.*

In many studies of the individual books in the Bible one verse is chosen as the Theme Verse or Most Important Verse. There seem to be two options for those who study Romans. Either Romans 1:16, which begins with "For I am not ashamed of the gospel, because it is the power of God that brings salvation . . . ," or Romans 12:1–2, the two verses that begin today's passage. First, there is no such most-important verse in Romans, nor does Paul tell us "This next set of lines are the most important in the whole letter." But let's admit it: discussing (and debating) which verse rises to the top often leads to insights into the whole letter. Readers who want to know the *purpose* of this letter may well find Romans 12:1–2 to be the most important because those verses provide a theoretical approach for how best to live in Rome as Christians.

Theme verses or not, today's passage is all about the body. Your body. Our body.

A Body for God

Romans 1–4 and 5–8 and 9–11—all summed up in "in view of God's mercy" (12:1), are now in the rearview mirror. Give a clap now to Phoebe for reading the letter at least five times aloud. Because the ideas of eleven chapters are now on the table, Paul can exhort the Romans to one simple way of life: *offer your bodies to God.* The word Paul uses for "offer" was often used for humans offering sacrifices in a temple or shrine, and many of the Romans would have (had) homes with an altar where simple offerings were presented.

The difference concerns *what* is offered. Now they are to offer their own bodies "as a living sacrifice," not one to be slaughtered. Their bodies become *everyday sacrifices.* Bodies offered to God become "holy and pleasing to God." We have a tendency to define "holy" with half of its meaning. Many will say "holy" means separate from common life, and that is true, but the sacrifice of our body only becomes holy *because it is devoted to and offered to the God who is holy, bringing our bodies into the circle of divine holiness.* Only when devoted to God does it get separated from common life (McKnight, *Five Things,* 116–148). Offering our bodies also becomes our "calculated veneration" or, as the NIV has it, our "true and proper worship" (12:1).

The words are a bit tricky. The word I translate "calculated" is *logikos,* and you can see it sounds like "logical." Which is one of the ideas expressed with this word, as is also "reasonable." The word I translate "veneration" refers to the acts of religious worship done for the good of the city, its leaders, and its people. Since "worship" morphs right away into singing time in our churches on Sunday morning, or what we do when we are having our private time or daily quiet time or devotions, I prefer a term that sticks out a little more. So I chose "veneration."

The positive side is the body-to-God offering. Paul flips the positive over to reveal the negative side of offering our bodies to God with "do not conform to the pattern of this world." The second half of holy (separation) here comes into view. Paul urges the believer to become separate from the ways of life in the here and now (12:2). The NIV's use of "world" can be translated more accurately as "this era" or "the present period of time in the plan of God." The word is *aiōn* and points to life in the here and now, which contrasts with life in the future, endless era we call eternal life or the kingdom of God.

Having turned body-to-God over to see body-away-from the here and now, Paul flips it back to the positive side with more about the body-to-God offering. Devoting the body to God promotes a "revival of the mind" (my translation) that remodels and transforms each of us. This everyday sacrifice leading to a remodeled body discovers, through the Spirit, new moral powers of discernment to know what is God's "good, pleasing, and perfect will" (12:2).

The body, as we can now see, includes the whole person: skin and bones and face and hair and mind and will and spirit. Paul summons the Romans to offer every globule of their being to God.

A Body for Others

Instructions about our body and my body morph into a different body, namely, the Body of Christ (12:3–8). Each of us is to see ourselves in light of how we fit in the Body of Christ (12:3). Each of us is a part of the one body, our local Body of

Christ (12:4–5). The language about *body parts* now morphs into the language about spiritual gifts, or Spirit-prompted contributions each of us make to the Body of Christ (12:6–8). Notice that a Spirit-prompted "gift" is just that: a *grace-act* given by God through the Spirit to the Body of Christ. These are not our accomplishments, but God's gifts. Gifts done by humans with their bodies. Unlike the world where competition reigns, where there are losers and winners, and where many are neglected, *everyone is a gift and a contribution to the Body of Christ*. There are no losers; there are no winners; there are only mutual donors.

The list of gifts in Romans 12:6–8 is like and unlike other lists (1 Corinthians 12:7–10, 27–30; Ephesians 4:11–12). Because the lists differ, we are wise not to make any of the lists the official list of gifts. Adding them together doesn't arrive at the official list either. Rather, the individual gifts, whatever they may be, are *symptoms and signs of what the Spirit is prompting each of us to do for the good of the Body of Christ*. Over time these gifts will vary from church to church, from context to context, from century to century. It's hard for me not to include the gift of writing or singing from a spiritual gift just because they are not on one of Paul's lists. Why do we need to squeeze singing—name your favorite Christian artist—into the gift of "encouragement"? Why not say it is a gift because God gave such a gift to Lauren Daigle? How many of us would say our faith was built up by reading books written by, say, Robert Chao Romero or Anne Lamott? Your gift is whatever contribution you make to those around you and in your church.

Paul has a concise word for the seven gifts he mentions in Romans 12. Two examples: if your gift is giving, "give generously," and if it is leading, "do it diligently" (or seriously) (12:8). As more gifts could have been listed, so more could have been said about how to exercise each.

A Body for the Church and the Public

At verse nine Paul launches a long list of exhortations. Verses nine through thirteen are for how believers should act within the Body of Christ, while verses fourteen through twenty-one turn toward the public. Remember 12:1–2: what Paul urges the believers to do in the rest of chapter twelve is what they are to do *in bodies offered to God, to one another, and to everyone they encounter.*

The primary concerns for life in the Body are: loving one another above all, being good especially in relations with one another (so far as it is possible), doing what is right, avoiding the status-mongering so common in the Roman empire, living in dependence on the Spirit and in interdependence with one another.

The primary concerns for life in the public sector are: eschewing retribution and vengeance, being empathic toward others, avoiding (again) the status-mongering temptations, and especially being peacemakers as much as is possible. This peacemaking theme can be found in the following verses: 12:16, 17, 18–21. Peace rises to the top of his concerns because (1) the believers are at odds with one another and they need to get that settled, (2) they are a minority in danger of getting the whole church in trouble, and (3) the way of Christ was peace and they are called to implement that now in every sphere of their lives.

War is easier than peace. As Marilynne's Robinson's character pastor John Ames expresses our proclivities toward war and vengeance, and thus to more vengeance and more war:

> . . . the desire for war would bring the consequences of war, because there is no ocean big enough to protect us from the Lord's judgment when we decide to hammer

> our plowshares into swords and our pruning hooks into spears in contempt of the will and the grace of God (Robinson, *Gilead*, 42).

Are we, am I, are you known for converting plowshares into swords or swords into plowshare.

Peace is central to discipleship. It is, sad to say, neglected by many who teach discipleship. Please read through these verses carefully and slowly to see the vitality of peace in Christian discipleship:

> **Luke 1:79** to shine on those living in darkness and in the shadow of death, to guide our feet into the path of peace.

> **Luke 2:14** Glory to God in the highest heaven, and on earth peace to those on whom his favor rests.

> **Matt. 5:9** Blessed are the peacemakers, for they will be called children of God.

> **Luke 10:5–6** When you enter a house, first say, 'Peace to this house.' [6] If someone who promotes peace is there, your peace will rest on them; if not, it will return to you.

> **Luke 19:38** "Blessed is the king who comes in the name of the Lord! Peace in heaven and glory in the highest!"

> **Luke 19:42** [Jesus said:] "If you, even you, had only known on this day what would bring you peace—but now it is hidden from your eyes.

> **Acts 10:36** [Peter, summarizing the gospel of Jesus:] You know the message God sent to the people of Israel,

announcing the good news of peace through Jesus Christ, who is Lord of all.

James 3:18 Peacemakers who sow in peace reap a harvest of righteousness.

And, too, Paul begins and ends nearly every letter with the word peace being used. We could add many more verses, but these are enough. The New Testament–from Jesus to John–urges those who follow Jesus to be peacemakers. So important is peace in the public sector that Paul is not done with it. He will now develop how believers are to relate to the government officials in Rome (13:1–7).

Questions for Reflection and Application

1. What did Romans 12:1–2 communicate to the churches about how to live in faith and unity in Rome?

2. What does it mean to make ourselves living sacrifices to God?

3. How does it impact your understanding of spiritual gifts to see them as "grace-acts"?

4. Have you ever taken a spiritual gifts test or inventory? How does that specific listing differ from the broader view of gifts given here?

5. What place does peace have in your understanding of discipleship? How can you increase its importance in your practice?

FOR FURTHER READING

Scot McKnight, *Five Things Biblical Scholars Wish Theologians Knew* (Downers Grove: IVP Academic, 2021).

Marilynne Robinson, *Gilead: A Novel* (New York: Farrar, Straus and Giroux, 2004).

GOVERNMENT AUTHORITIES AND REDEMPTIVE PEACE

Romans 13:1–7

[1] Let everyone be subject to the governing authorities, for there is no authority except that which God has established. The authorities that exist have been established by God.

[2] Consequently, whoever rebels against the authority is rebelling against what God has instituted, and those who do so will bring judgment on themselves. [3] For rulers hold no terror for those who do right, but for those who do wrong. Do you want to be free from fear of the one in authority? Then do what is right and you will be commended. [4] For the one in authority is God's servant for your good. But if you do wrong, be afraid, for rulers do not bear the sword for no reason. They are God's servants, agents of wrath to bring punishment on the wrongdoer. [5] Therefore, it is necessary to submit to the authorities, not only because of possible punishment but also as a matter of conscience.

[6] This is also why you pay taxes, for the authorities are God's servants, who give their full time to governing. [7] Give to everyone what you owe them: If you owe taxes, pay taxes; if revenue, then revenue; if respect, then respect; if honor, then honor.

If I worked in Washington, D.C., or in the State capitol building or in the local village's office, I'd love today's passage. I don't. If I were an oppressed person of color, if I were a woman in a masculinist employment culture, I would be wary of this passage. If I were a Christian in some part of the world filled with persecution, I would not like this passage. For one example, one could read with a small group Esau McCaulley's *Reading While Black*, an African American Bible scholar and clergy who writes about his experience of reading the Bible as a Black man. What he hears is not always what I (a white man) hear. One's attitude and posture toward this passage gains its form from the person's location on the social ladder. In the history of the church, whether by those in political power or by those with power over the enslaved, this passage has been used and abused with tragic results. All because of that person's social status and location, and all because those who suffered were where they were on the social status scale.

Romans 13 speaks to our social location, but our social location also speaks to Romans 13. I hope to show how.

Paul and Privilege

Paul had some privilege. He was a *Roman citizen* (Acts 25:11). The powerful Howard Thurman once said Paul was "a minority with majority privileges" (Thurman, *Jesus and the Disinherited,* 32). Yes, to be fully accurate, Paul experienced more than his share of suffering at the hands of Rome-based local political authorities (read 2 Corinthians 11:21–29). Let's be honest. It's much easier for a citizen to utter Romans 13:1 than for an enslaved mine worker.

His privilege as a citizen was not the only factor, however, that led him to open Romans 13 with these words: "Let everyone be subject to the governing authorities" because these "authorities that exist have been established by God" (13:1). His *mission* shaped those words. Put differently, he had a strategy of being good so we can avoid trouble and continue with the gospel work. A mission posture does not erase the damage that can be done by pushing Romans 13:1 into the pulpit of those who are suffering at the hands of the "governing authorities." The Bible knows full well of instances, not least Acts 4:20, where we read of Peter telling Jerusalem's Rome-appointed authorities that "we cannot help speaking about what we have seen and heard" and they continued their gospel work in the face of opposition from the governing authorities. Location determines posture but so does *timing.*

What is being asked of a citizen also matters. Paul's idea of "be subject" then was determined by what the authorities were demanding. If they demanded no preaching of the gospel, Paul would not "be subject." To mess with English, he would "be subvert." Romans 13:1–7, which looks like blanket endorsement, almost certainly reflects some concern Paul has with *what was going on in Rome* with some of the believers. Some were pondering levels of subversion that Paul thought was not only unnecessary but also dangerous for the Christian church.

Paul and Context

A quick reminder. Paul's letter was not drafted with chapter divisions. Romans 13:1–7 fits into a larger section, Romans 12–13. Romans 13 follows hard on a passage that was concerned with pursuing peace with everyone and not being vindictive but instead being peaceful and good (12:14–21). Then, too, 13:1–7 leads into a passage about the single Christian debt: loving one's neighbor as oneself (13:8–10). If we read 13:1–7 as *a call to peace and a call to love,* we read the passage afresh. Instead of a heavy-handed, top-down, hierarchical demand of submission, Paul offers a peace-and-love submission for how to live in Rome as followers of Jesus. That may not answer all the difficulties of this text, but it sure does offer a fresh and more context-shaped angle. One more word about context: those who read Romans 13 need also to read Revelation. Romans 13 and Revelation 13 are about Rome. One says be a good citizen and the other says resist the empire! Each passage speaking in its day in its way.

God and the Authorities: Five Observations

We draw your attention to the following: (1) God is above and under all political powers (13:1, 2, 4, 5). When Paul says "conscience" in 13:5 he's talking about consciousness of God. (2) The divine design for all "governing authorities" is "for your good," that is for safety and justice and peace (13:4). When the rulers cease being servants of God for the good of the people, they lose authority and rest under God's judgment. Martin Luther King, Jr., in his famous letter from jail, urged his listeners to obey just laws and to disobey unjust laws–and those who implement the unjust laws (King, "Letter," 293). (3) The verb "rebels" in 13:2 is about anarchy and chaos and even social or armed rebellion. This clarifies the passage because we are not talking about preaching the gospel but intentional rebellion. Like the attack on the Capitol on January 6, not like the Civil Rights Movement. (4) Rebellion against Rome will lead to Rome's military might overpowering the rebels. Paul describes Rome's might as "judgment" on the rebels doing "wrong" (13:2–5). (5) In this context the instruction to "be subject" (13:1) or "submit" (13:5) cannot mean blanket endorsement or do whatever they say no matter what they ask.

Paul worries about reckless political and social revolts. In such actions the believers—first century, Rome, small house churches, etc.—are not to engage. They are to do good, to be good, and to stay clear of trouble for the sake of the gospel—but they will preach the gospel if it costs them their lives. It is well-known that the apostle Paul got to Rome and was executed for his missionary work among the gentiles.

God and the Taxes

Surprise. Paul suddenly instructs the Powerful and probably even more the Powerless to pay taxes. Maybe some in Rome, perhaps the Powerless (as I think more likely), have heard Jesus' words about Caesar's coin. Perhaps they heard Jesus saying it's all God's, and so they thought they'd not have to pay taxes. On top of this there were at times extra taxes for those who moved into Rome from other regions of the empire.

Today's passage leaves us with enough unknowables for us to exercise caution. Perhaps the rebellion and revolution-type language of 13:1–5 was, in the end, only about their refusal to pay these (extra?) taxes. Maybe then "be subject" and "submit" are about paying taxes. Maybe the governing authorities are the revenue collectors. What we can say with some confidence is that not paying taxes was a symbolic act of resistance and, for the governing authorities, was tantamount to official rebellion. Paul believes they ought to pay the taxes.

Paying taxes embodies the redemptive peace that forges unity among believers and respect from those with social authority.

Questions for Reflection and Application

1. What is your social location in the world, and how does that impact how you feel about today's passage?

2. How do Paul's mission and circumstance inform his teaching here?

3. Why does Paul address paying taxes?

4. How do you discern when it is the right time to be a good citizen and when it is the right time to resist the empire?

5. How can you live with a stronger sense of redemptive peace in your social location?

FOR FURTHER READING

Martin Luther King, Jr., "Letter from Birmingham Jail," in *A Testament of Hope: The Essential Writings of Martin Luther King, Jr.*, ed. James M. Washington (San Francisco: Harper and Row, 1986).

Esau McCaulley, *Reading While Black: African American Biblical Interpretation as an Exercise in Hope* (Downers Grove: IVP Academic, 2020).

Howard Thurman, *Jesus and the Disinherited* (Richmond, Indiana: Friends United, 1981).

LOVE IN THE PRESENT SEASON OF REDEMPTIVE PEACE

Romans 13:8–14

[8] Let no debt remain outstanding, except the continuing debt to love one another, for whoever loves others has fulfilled the law. [9] The commandments, "You shall not commit adultery," "You shall not murder," "You shall not steal," "You shall not covet," and whatever other command there may be, are summed up in this one command: "Love your neighbor as yourself." [10] Love does no harm to a neighbor. Therefore love is the fulfillment of the law.

[11] And do this, understanding the present time: The hour has already come for you to wake up from your slumber, because our salvation is nearer now than when we first believed. [12] The night is nearly over; the day is almost here. So let us put aside the deeds of darkness and put on the armor of light. [13] Let us behave decently, as in the daytime, not in carousing and drunkenness, not in sexual immorality and debauchery, not in dissension and jealousy. [14] Rather, clothe yourselves with the Lord Jesus Christ, and do not think about how to gratify the desires of the flesh.

Without paragraph divisions with headers separating verses, we would more easily see the subtle shift from "give" and "owe" in 13:7 to "debt" in 13:8. The terms behind each English word vary but they all belong in the tax auditor's little purse. A shift already occurred in verse six from paying taxes to paying social dues, namely, "respect" and "honor." Shifting from citizen obligations to social virtues opens Paul's mind to the biggest debt of all.

Taxes pale in value and virtue to love, just as Caesar pales in importance to God. What God wants matters most. Paul must already have in mind what he's about to tell the Powerful and Powerless in Romans 14–15, namely, love one another by welcoming one another. (Because of the importance of those two chapters to the whole of Romans, we discussed them early in this study guide (pp. 5–21).)

Love:
Three Observations

Because of Jesus, our first observation is that love became the central virtue in the Pauline mission churches (Romans 13:8, 10). One needs only to read 1 Corinthians 13 along with Galatians 5:14 and Colossians 3:14 to observe the glue love can become. Love, again, is a rugged, affective commitment to another person in a relationship that involves presence with one another, support of one another, and mutual growth in Christlikeness. Love like this spreads peace among the redeemed.

Paul believes, second, that loving one another *fills up* the whole the law of Moses. Jesus famously reduced the law of Moses to loving God and loving others (Mark 12:28–34), what I call the "Jesus Creed." All the laws, some 365 in the first five books of Moses, are observed by the person who has learned to love their neighbor. Those laws are not done away with. Instead, each law expresses what it means to love others (or God). The word behind "fulfilled" (13:8, 10), *plērōma*, appears in Paul for the full number of both Jewish and gentile believers (11:12, 25), for the blessing of Christ (15:29), for the plan of history coming to its fullness in Christ (Galatians 4:4), for the unity that comes in Christ at the end of time (Ephesians 1:10; 4:13), and it is used for the expansive, extensive, and unlimited fulfillment in one person, namely Jesus Christ (1:23; Colossians 1:9; 2:9). Love does not replace the law of Moses; it does not cut the first half of our Bibles out. Instead, the one who loves fills up and fills out and fills in what the laws were all about.

And third, the one who loves their neighbor "does not harm to a neighbor" (Romans 13:10). Love's commitment to the other means a believer does not work in such way that another experiences evil from them. The NIV's "does no harm" is perhaps too soft. The term points to behaviors that are bad, evil, corrupted, and intended to wound and destroy. I got two letters this week from leaders in churches who had been deeply wounded by the lies of the senior pastor about them, lies that were told to destroy their reputation. Paul has such behaviors in mind. One cannot love a person and lie about the person in order to discredit them.

Time:
Three Observations

In turning to the "present time" Paul shifts topics once again. He has not discussed time, or what we call eschatology, with any emphasis so far in this lengthy letter. Yet this early Christian sense of time as the kingdom of now-and-not-yet lurks under every chapter in the New Testament. God has acted afresh in Jesus—in his kingdom message—and in the Spirit—in the Spirit's arrival. So fresh is the newness that Paul can say "the new creation has come . . . the new is here" (2 Corinthians 5:17). Jesus and the apostles all taught a singular idea: the new day has arrived, but the fullness of that day is yet to come. Michael Gorman's way of putting this, which I really like, is that Paul has a "bifocal" vision: one eye on the first coming and another eye on the second coming (Gorman, *Apostle of the Crucified Lord,* 183).

Notice how Paul frames it in Romans 13:11–14. First, he wants them to understand the *season* (NIV: "present time"; 13:11). Our church observes the church calendar, and each Sunday occupies a slot in a season, and the seasons make up the church year. Paul expands the seasons of a calendar to think cosmically. We all are in the massive plan of God for the history of everything (8:18–30). The season they are in begins when they wake up from the slumbering in sin and the flesh (13:14; Galatians 1:4) by turning in faith to Jesus as the Lord. They are both already saved and still awaiting the fulness of salvation (Romans 13:11). Second, a season of night or darkness shrouds this season of believers being awake. Darkness will eventually surrender to the brightness of the Last Day, and surely he is thinking of the Day of Christ's return (13:12). In this present season of darkness, the believers are to live as if they are living in the future kingdom. They are to wear the "armor of light" and to live respectable lives (NIV: "behave decently"), the kind of behaviors done in the daylight. Those behaviors contrast with the carousings of the night, and Rome was known for night debaucheries (13:13). Third, the believers are to live like Christ, that is, to "clothe yourselves with the Lord Jesus Christ" (13:14). Many think such clothing evokes post-baptismal robes worn by fresh converts. Perhaps so.

Questions for Reflection and Application

1. How does love spread peace in churches?

2. How does love fulfill the law?

3. What does it mean to be already saved and yet awaiting the fulness of salvation?

4. Have you ever been part of or even visited a church that followed the liturgical calendar? How did that impact your understanding of seasons and times?

5. What would it look like for you to live as if you were in the future kingdom of light, while you are still present in our current time of darkness?

FOR FURTHER READING

Michael Gorman, *Apostle of the Crucified Lord: A Theological Introduction to Paul and His Letters,* 2d ed.; Grand Rapids: Wm. B. Eerdmans, 2017).

Marilynne Robinson, *Home: A Novel* (New York: Farrar, Straus and Giroux, 2008). Those who love her novels will want to read the novel about that son, a novel called *Jack* (New York: Farrar, Straus and Giroux, 2020).

Note to the Reader: For the study guide discussing Romans 14:1–23 see pp. 5–21.

ACCEPTANCE OF OTHERS PROMOTES REDEMPTIVE PEACE

Romans 15:1–13

[1] We who are strong ought to bear with the failings of the weak and not to please ourselves.

[2] Each of us should please our neighbors for their good, to build them up. [3] For even Christ did not please himself but, as it is written: "The insults of those who insult you have fallen on me." [4] For everything that was written in the past was written to teach us, so that through the endurance taught in the Scriptures and the encouragement they provide we might have hope.

[5] May the God who gives endurance and encouragement give you the same attitude of mind toward each other that Christ Jesus had, [6] so that with one mind and one voice you may glorify the God and Father of our Lord Jesus Christ.

[7] Accept one another, then, just as Christ accepted you, in order to bring praise to God. [8] For I tell you that Christ has become a servant of the Jews on behalf of God's truth, so that the promises made to the patriarchs might be confirmed [9] and, moreover, that the Gentiles might glorify God for his mercy. As it is written:

"Therefore I will praise you among the Gentiles;
I will sing the praises of your name."
[10] *Again, it says,*
"Rejoice, you Gentiles, with his people."
[11] *And again,*
"Praise the Lord, all you Gentiles;
let all the peoples extol him."
[12] *And again, Isaiah says,*
"The Root of Jesse will spring up, one who will arise to rule over the nations; in him the Gentiles will hope."

[13] *May the God of hope fill you with all joy and peace as you trust in him, so that you may overflow with hope by the power of the Holy Spirit.*

In the text above the underlined words indicate Paul's audience. The passage starts with "We who are" the Powerful (15:1), but he then shifts to everyone. To indicate that shift, the term changes from the Powerful to "each of us" and "each other" and "one another." The shifts in audience do not change the vision Paul has for their peaceful unity. Divisions are the problem. As Sarah Lancaster puts it so clearly, "Fractious factions not only tear churches apart and cause pain to individuals in those churches, they also destroy the evidence of the dominion of grace as alternative to the dominion of sin" (Lancaster, *Romans*, 251). Like Paul, she sees our present life in cosmic terms.

For the Powerful: Solidarity, Not Superiority

I urge you to skim through Romans 14 again to catch a good feel for the Powerful, those (probably) gentile believers who exploited both their freedom from the law of Moses and their status compared with the Powerless. They believed they ought to be in charge of the house churches in Rome. Paul identifies himself with the Powerful (for the moment), though we'd be mistaken to think their arrogance was permissible. Rather, their practice of the law matched his.

The instructions for those who think they have power and authority in a church, for those who have experienced freedom (of various types), and for those with a sense of high status are these: "Accept the one whose faith is weak" and avoid "quarreling over disputable matters" (14:1), don't "treat with the contempt" (14:3), "bear with the" *weaknesses of the powerless* and don't become self-pleasers (15:1; the NIV's "failings" misses the social status connection at work). In our terms, "get over your high and mighty selves and what you think about your freedoms." Put differently, show respect for others. Accommodate yourself to others. Don't merely tolerate them but learn their perspective, wear their practices some, and value them as fellow image-bearers who have a different view. Shoulder their load with them. Get off your perch and join them. He urges "*solidarity* rather than . . . *superiority*" (Gorman, *Romans*, 277, italics are his). Paul sees both sides as believers who are redeemed by the same Savior and brought together into the Savior's same Body, the church. In that fellowship they can seek fellowship that transcends difference and forms into a unity of peace.

Such Are His Prayers

Redemptive peace and unity is the prayer of Paul. In both Romans 15:5–6 and 15:13, Paul prays for the believers in Rome. He prays for the kind of unity that flows from redemptive peace into praising God (15:5–6), and he prays that God will "fill" them with "joy and peace" as they learn to be faithful to God. A life of joy, peace, and allegiant faith will flourish into "hope by the power of the Holy Spirit" (15:13).

Notice in today's passage that the themes of unity and peace pop up often. Knowing that Paul's pastoral concerns are the factions forming around the leaders of the Powerful and the Powerless, it is no surprise that peace and unity are at the front of his instructions.

In our church, each Sunday we have a time called "Passing the Peace." We say, "Peace of Christ" and the other person says, "And to you" or "Peace of Christ." I once greeted a visitor with "Peace of Christ," and he gave me a "Same to you, buddy!" Not quite up to form for our church, but it got the message across just the same.

For Everyone: Be like Jesus

Which leads Paul once again to everyone, and his fundamental instruction for all the believers is "accept one another" (15:7) as an act of learning to "please our neighbors" in a way that leads to their spiritual formation, that is, to what is good (15:2). Accepting and pleasing the other appears as well in Jesus' famous love your neighbor creed (Mark 12:28–34) and in the Golden Rule (Matthew 7:12). Easier to affirm than to live when it matters the most. Another way of framing it is to speak of self-denial (Luke 9:23). Everybody needs to live like Christ. The Powerless may be looking across the room at the Powerful, and the Powerful at the Powerless. Phoebe is moving her eyes between groups.

Loving the other, whether Powerful or Powerless, discovers its model in Jesus himself. Not in Paul, not in Peter, not in Mary, not in Phoebe. First, "even Christ did not please himself" but endured the cross for the sake of others, and he quotes words from Psalm 69:9 to deepen the way of Christ (Romans 15:3). Second, his prayer was to have the attitude that Christ had, (15:5) and third, their ready reception of one another discovers its model in Christ, too. He has "accepted you" (15:7). Once again Paul states that the essence of true life before God is the life of Christ. God redeems in order to morph humans into the image of his Son (8:29). The Spirit is transforming (8:1–4) and the mind is being transformed (12:1–12), but the aim is Christoformity (15:3, 7).

Paul deepens Christ's acceptance of believers by appealing to Christ's role as a servant to the circumcised (15:8; NIV has "Jews"). Which leads Paul to display his memory of Bible verses.

For Gentiles

With gentiles now swarming into the people of God in record numbers. Their inclusion required an explanation. Paul's explanation is the Bible's: from the beginning God planned to include gentiles in the people of God (Genesis 12:3), and that time is now. Easy explanations, however, often do not lead to easy transformations of groups.

Remember how Paul said his mission was "first to the Jew, then to the Gentile" (1:16; 2:9)? He's making the same observation here. But this time it's Jesus's mission. Jesus was a servant to the Jews *so that the gospel would expand to the gentiles,* just as the promises to Abraham announced (Genesis 12:3). In every synagogue or street corner Paul preached both the inclusion of gentiles and the non-necessity of their becoming Torah observant. In each of those locations Paul got pushback for having a cavalier attitude toward the law; that is, just like the Powerful, he preached a kind of freedom from the law. Paul himself practiced that same freedom (1 Corinthians 9:19–23). But his practice was intentional, not cavalier.

The Pauline mission was to include gentiles. That mission derived from the Bible itself. One has to think as Paul read the Scriptures or heard it read in synagogues, that he began to collect lines that supported his gentile mission—beside the experience of God telling him to preach to the gentiles (Acts 9:15). He committed to memory the following verses that he quotes in Romans 15:9–12: either 2 Samuel 22:50 or Psalm 18:49, which are identical verses, and Deuteronomy 32:43, and Psalm 117:1 and Isaiah 11:10. These verses affirm praising God among gentiles, the invitation of gentiles to join the praise of Israel's God, and the turning of gentiles to hope in Israel's God.

His mission to the gentiles is entirely biblical!

Questions for Reflection and Application

1. Re-read the first verse of today's passage. The CEB translates it, "We who are powerful need to be patient with the weakness of those who don't have power." What does the different translation do for your understanding of the verse?

2. What does Paul ask God for in his prayers for the churches in Rome?

3. How did Jesus model not pleasing himself before Paul asked the Roman Christians to follow the same practice?

4. On what pre-existing plan of God did Paul build his mission to the gentiles?

5. How can you move beyond tolerating those whose beliefs are different from yours and truly value them?

THE MUNDANE IN REDEMPTIVE PEACE

Romans 15:14–33

[14] I myself am convinced, my brothers and sisters, that you yourselves are full of goodness, filled with knowledge and competent to instruct one another. [15] Yet I have written you quite boldly on some points to remind you of them again, because of the grace God gave me [16] to be a minister of Christ Jesus to the Gentiles. He gave me the priestly duty of proclaiming the gospel of God, so that the Gentiles might become an offering acceptable to God, sanctified by the Holy Spirit.

[17] Therefore I glory in Christ Jesus in my service to God. [18] I will not venture to speak of anything except what Christ has accomplished through me in leading the Gentiles to obey God by what I have said and done—[19] by the power of signs and wonders, through the power of the Spirit of God. So from Jerusalem all the way around to Illyricum, I have fully proclaimed the gospel of Christ. [20] It has always been my ambition to preach the gospel where Christ was not known, so that I would not be building on someone else's foundation. [21] Rather, as it is written:

> *"Those who were not told about him will see,*
> *and those who have not heard will understand."*

[22] This is why I have often been hindered from coming to you.

[23] But now that there is no more place for me to work in these regions, and since I have been longing for many years to visit you, [24] I plan to do so when I go to Spain. I hope to see you while passing through and to have you assist me on my journey there, after I have enjoyed your company for a while.

[25] Now, however, I am on my way to Jerusalem in the service of the Lord's people there. [26] For Macedonia and Achaia were pleased to make a contribution for the poor among the Lord's people in Jerusalem. [27] They were pleased to do it, and indeed they owe it to them. For if the Gentiles have shared in the Jews' spiritual blessings, they owe it to the Jews to share with them their material blessings. [28] So after I have completed this task and have made sure that they have received this contribution, I will go to Spain and visit you on the way. [29] I know that when I come to you, I will come in the full measure of the blessing of Christ.

[30] I urge you, brothers and sisters, by our Lord Jesus Christ and by the love of the Spirit, to join me in my struggle by praying to God for me. [31] Pray that I may be kept safe from the unbelievers in Judea and that the contribution I take to Jerusalem may be favorably received by the Lord's people there, [32] so that I may come to you with joy, by God's will, and in your company be refreshed. [33] The God of peace be with you all. Amen.

Life involves lots of the mundane. Plans for the whole year, plans for the quarter, plans for the school year. Plans for children, for the youth, and at church for the worship and music teams. Plans for what is local and national and international. Plans for the budget, plans for decorating, plans for coffee, plans for lunch, plans for a podcast, plans to go running. At church, plans for the sanctuary and the classrooms and the offices and the vestibule and the front and the sides and the back and the parking lot. Plans for job descriptions and vacations and renewal and retreats. And then there are relationships, some good, some not so good, and some awful. On top of all this, for anyone involved, is the burden of nurturing Christlikeness at every level for everyone committed to Christ. Plans here and plans there and plans everywhere. So much of it seems mundane.

In the mundane our spirituality is formed. People praying while cooking or driving or doing the dishes or mowing the grass or shoveling the snow. Paul knows lots about the mundane. Kathleen Norris, in a book with a title looking with eyes wide open at the mundane, a book called *The Quotidian Mysteries: Laundry, Liturgy and "Women's Work,"* says at one point, "The Bible is full of evidence that God's attention is indeed fixed on the little things." If you have ever taught Leviticus, and I have, you may appreciate her writing about the "ludicrous attention to details in the book of Leviticus"! I sure do (Norris, 21, 22). In life's mundane, ordinary details we are formed spiritually. Churches obsessed with the biggest shows of the calendar year—like Christmas and Easter—can neglect the ordinary Sundays filled with ordinary days and ordinary people. During ordinary times ordinary people are spiritually formed.

These Everyday Bible Study guides are designed for our quotidian realities, the mundane act of opening your Bible, reading a passage, and reflecting on it with me. More growth takes place over time doing the mundane than attending some hot-shot preacher's or band's special event.

As Paul's letters wound down, they frequently turned to mundane topics like his plans. Read 1 Corinthians 16:5–18 for an example. Being the long letter that Romans is, Paul's winding down takes longer—most of two chapters before he signs the final line with a hearty Amen! (15:16–16:27). Today's passage explains Paul's mundane-planned mission to the gentiles with a rare (for him) image, then he reveals to the Romans his plans to move on to Spain. Before Spain, however, he needs to return to Jerusalem to deliver the monies he has collected for the poor believers there. His deep concerns about his own safety, spoken of here for the only time, proved to be more than justified. He was arrested, put on trial for a couple years, and then finally sent off to Rome as a prisoner. Many think he was freed, perhaps preached in Spain, and then resumed his ministry in Ephesus—only to be arrested again and executed.

Paul's letters often find the keys for his most pastoral chords. Paul assures the Romans of his confidence in them—after his long letter with more than a few strong expressions. He is "convinced" that they are "full of goodness" (15:14–15). The way to win your audience, according to Roman and Greek teachings about rhetoric, begins by affirming your audience. Paul fit right in with these words, and his audience's norm was respected.

His Gentile Mission

Paul's ministry image, to begin with, was that of a priest. Many today think priest belongs to the Catholics and Orthodox and Anglicans but not to the Protestant branches of the church. Going by what church folk call their pastor, they're right. But they're not biblical. Paul knew he was called by God to mediate between people and God, and every pastor worth her or his salt knows they mediate. Just like ancient priests. The pastoral role comes to its purest expression in its priestly role. Paul's language explicitly evokes priesting and such terms are italicized: "because of the grace God gave me to be a *minister* of Christ Jesus to the Gentiles. He gave me *the priestly duty* of proclaiming the gospel of God, so that the Gentiles might become *an offering* acceptable to God, *sanctified* by the Holy Spirit" (15:15–16). No verse in the New Testament is this priest-drenched. A priest takes a worshiper's offering and offers it to God in worship, assuring the offer-er that God's redemptive work is accomplished.

What can't be ignored because it only comes to the surface a few verses later is that the "offering" Paul will present, with the hope of an affirmative reception by the church leaders in Jerusalem, is money (15:25–28). We call this the Pauline collection for the saints (see 1 Corinthians 16:1–3). It was one of the most mundane features of Paul's mission. Something mundane, perhaps, but filled with symbolic power. The NIV's addition in italics in Romans 15: "an offering acceptable *to God*," misses the importance of a very difficult social reality. What was at stake was not God's acceptance. Paul knew God approved of the funds given by the gentiles. What was at stake was whether the Jerusalem church leaders would accept the gift. Accepting that gift would embody approval of the Pauline mission to the gentiles, a mission they all knew did not require gentile converts to observe the law.

Not only was his ministry a priestly offering of funds in Jerusalem, that same ministry was reduced to speaking about nothing "except what Christ has accomplished through me in leading the Gentiles to obey God by what I have said and done" (15:18). All the great wonders and miracles, Paul quickly confesses, is the work of "the Spirit of God" (15:19). Wherever he has been, from "Jerusalem all the way around to Illyricum" (east coast of the Adriatic Sea), all he's done is gospel here and gospel there. He loves to go "where Christ was not known" so as to avoid crossing wires with other apostles and gospelers (15:20). Here is a fact that puts the "where Christ was not known" into context. Paul's central location for his gospel mission was Ephesus. Not Jerusalem, not Antioch, not Athens or Corinth or Thessalonica, and certainly not Rome. We know that the apostle John had a ministry in Ephesus (cf. Revelation 2:1–7), and that also Mary, mother of Jesus, probably lived there. Paul's mission work in

Galatia was quickly countered by some Jerusalem-based mission workers "from James" according to Galatians 2:11–14. The various messages to the seven churches of Western Asia Minor in Revelation 2–3 indicate, too, that other teachers had risen to some significance. Even if they were misguided, Paul was not alone.

His Spanish Plans

Amazingly, Paul thinks he's "done" Asia Minor and Greece and is ready to skip Rome, since others have done mission work there, and head off to Spain (15:23–24; 28–29). We don't know for sure if Paul ever got there. Clement of Rome, a later writer, said Paul "served as a herald in both the East and the West," and most think Clement is referring to Spain (*1 Clement* 5:6, LCL 24, trans. Bart D. Ehrman).

His Concerns about Jerusalem

More pressing than his mundane plans is what he fears could happen in Jerusalem when he arrives with his bountiful collection for the poor believers there. Paul spent some two decades raising funds. The donors are from Galatia (1 Corinthians 16:1), Derbe and Lystra and Berea and Thessalonica (Acts 16:1; 20:4), from Macedonia and Achaia (2 Corinthians 8:1–5; 9:2, 4; Romans 15:26), from Philippi (Acts 16:12, 16; 20:6), from Corinth (Romans 15:26; 1 Corinthians 16:1–4), and probably from Mysia and Ephesus (Acts 20:4), and Troas (20:5–6). And probably from nearly every other city mentioned in his letters. Paul believes the gentile mission churches have a material obligation to Jerusalem for the spiritual blessing and gift Jerusalem has provided in the Messiah (Romans 15:27).

There is an undeniable and noteworthy silence in Acts 21:17–26 about the reception of the collection. It pains me there's no celebration about this collection. It was so important to Paul. Still, in his trial before Felix, Paul says he gave alms for the people of Jerusalem (24:17). Perhaps they accepted his gift, perhaps they didn't. What we do know is that Paul got in trouble right away after arriving, and that he seemed to get no help from the major Jerusalem leaders then nor during his lengthy captivity in Caesarea.

Paul anticipated opposition but wanted reception for his gift so he could come to Rome emotionally and missionally satisfied. For these concerns he asked the Romans to pray for him (Romans 15:30–33).

The mundane is the location of spiritual formation.

Questions for Reflection and Application

1. How did Paul function as a priest?

2. Why was Paul concerned about the reception of the offering in Jerusalem?

3. Why did Paul plan to travel to Spain?

4. How have you experienced your Christlikeness being shaped during the mundane parts of life?

5. As you near the end of this Study Guide, reflect on your time in Romans with this book. How has your steady faithfulness to return here again and again shaped you over time?

FOR FURTHER READING

Kathleen Norris, *The Quotidian Mysteries: Laundry, Liturgy and "Women's Work"* (New York: Paulist, 1998).

Note to the Reader: For the study guide discussing Romans 16:1–16, see pp. 22–29.

ENDING A LETTER ABOUT REDEMPTIVE PEACE

Romans 16:17–27

[17] I urge you, brothers and sisters, to watch out for those who cause divisions and put obstacles in your way that are contrary to the teaching you have learned. Keep away from them. [18] For such people are not serving our Lord Christ, but their own appetites. By smooth talk and flattery they deceive the minds of naive people. [19] Everyone has heard about your obedience, so I rejoice because of you; but I want you to be wise about what is good, and innocent about what is evil.

[20] The God of peace will soon crush Satan under your feet.

The grace of our Lord Jesus be with you.

[21] Timothy, my co-worker, sends his greetings to you, as do Lucius, Jason and Sosipater, my fellow Jews.

[22] I, Tertius, who wrote down this letter, greet you in the Lord.

[23] Gaius, whose hospitality I and the whole church here enjoy, sends you his greetings.

Erastus, who is the city's director of public works, and our brother Quartus send you their greetings.

[25] Now to him who is able to establish you in accordance with my gospel, the message I proclaim about Jesus Christ, in keeping with the revelation of the mystery hidden for long ages past, [26] but now revealed and made known through the prophetic writings by the command of the eternal God, so that all the Gentiles might come to the obedience that comes from faith—[27] to the only wise God be glory forever through Jesus Christ! Amen.

Romans is the longest and the most influential letter Paul wrote. More than that, Romans is the most influential document in the history of the church. We have not discussed the history of theology, nor am I qualified to do so, but the major voices that have shaped the entire history of what Christians believe have a theology nearly always rooted in Romans. Whole denominations have confessions rooted in Paul: Presbyterians, Methodists, Anglicans, Baptists, and others. Seminaries teach theology and form students into a way of thinking and living, and many of those seminaries are Paul-based, Romans-shaped theologies.

One has to wonder, however, if the redemptive peace theme of Romans could have made many of these centers of power more unified rather than divided. I don't wonder. I believe it could have done that, and it still can. Romans deserves a fresh reading, starting at the back.

Pastoral Ending

The ending of one of Paul's letters, like a beginning, often brings the most pressing issues into play. This one surely does. The issue is "divisions" and "obstacles" by people who are serving "their own appetites," people who are gifted enough speakers for Paul to say they have "smooth talk and flattery" and can "deceive the minds of naïve people." Unless Paul has somehow radically shifted concerns from Romans

14–15, we are pressed by this letter to see here the powers of the Powerful and the resisting powers of the Powerless. One might think of the Judge of Romans 2:1 or the haughtiness of the so-called Powerful.

I suspect it is both. What matters is not Who these divisive people are but the aim of Paul. He desires the unity and peace that flows from redemption, looks like Jesus' own way of life, and is empowered by the Spirit. In the span of two chapters Paul publicly affirms the Roman Christians for Christian character and behaviors. At 15:14 he affirmed their "goodness" and "knowledge" and their ability "to instruct one another," and now he publicly affirms their "obedience." He simply wants their Christian character to flow into being "wise" and "good" and "innocent about what is evil" (16:19). These are gentle words that frame a long and strong letter. Ending with such pastorally affirming words, words read aloud by Phoebe to each house church, will inspire the believers to live in peace with one another and become vigilant about divisive people. So he hopes. Don't you wonder what happened between the Powerful and Powerless when he finally arrived?

Some Loose Endings

We can experience the endings of apostles' letters as random final thoughts, but the promise at 16:20 is a beauty, random or not. "The God of peace," and we have to observe that the term "peace" echoes what he said about divisions in 16:17–19, "will"—how much more certain does it get!—"Soon crush Satan under your feet"—that's good news, and it echoes Genesis 3. The long-awaited defeat of the serpent who provoked sin into action is on the horizon. A fuller expression of this promise can be found in Ephesians 6:12.

Paul often prays for "grace" for his churches at the end of his letters. Look up 1 Corinthians 16:23–24, 2 Corinthians

13:14, Galatians 6:18, Ephesians 6:23–24, Philippians 4:23, Colossians 4:18, 1 Thessalonians 5:28, 2 Thessalonians 3:18, 1 Timothy 6:21, 2 Timothy 4:22, Titus 3:15, and Philemon 25. Paul always ends with grace, because for Paul the whole redemption and peace are through God's unending and powerful grace.

He often also mentions names of those who are with him when the letter is written and sent, and from these names we learn about Paul as team player who is surrounded by his "besties," his co-workers in the gospel mission to the gentiles. Here we learn about Timothy, Lucius, Jason, Sosipater, as well as three high status men named Gaius and Erastus and Quartus. These two indicate the letter derived from Corinth or its port city, Cenchreae.

Notice who actually "wrote down this letter." His name is Tertius. Paul was smart and educated but not a good writer. Which meant he was never trained in the skill of handwriting. He wrote this long letter by discussing it with the above names, and probably more, in the presence of Tertius. He then participated, probably with Timothy and maybe others, in dictating it to Tertius. Tertius then would have read what he wrote down, to which there were responses and corrections, and then he had a full rough draft, which was read again in front of Paul and others. Then with all the corrections in place, Paul signed off on a final draft, handed it to Phoebe, and off she went to Rome to read it and explain it.

Final Doxology

The final prayer benediction of Paul re-emphasizes one more time his mission from God to preach the gospel to the gentiles (16:25–26), and then gives all the glory to God (16:27). We call this a doxology because the Greek word for glory is *doxa*.

Amen?

Questions for Reflection and Application

1. How would you summarize Paul's letter to the Romans in one paragraph?

2. What positive affirmations does Paul give the Roman Christians?

3. What is most interesting to you about the composition process of Paul's letters?

4. How have Romans and Paul-focused theologies shaped the spiritual communities you have been a part of?

5. How has reading Romans backwards at times impacted your understanding of the letter?

NOTES

The Gospel Mission of Redemptive Peace

1. Acts 2:14–39; 3:12–26; 4:8–12; 10:34–43 with 11:4–18; 13:16–41; 14:15–17; 17:22–31.

Redemptive Peace Lives in Light of the Judgment

1. The NIV has a bad habit of turning the positive use of "works" in the NT to words like "deeds" or in this passage to "what they have done" (2:6). The word in the quotation from the Old Testament is "works" (*erga*), which can be used positively or negatively, depending on context.

Abraham's God and Redemptive Peace

1. Romans 4:1 could be two questions: What are we to say then?, as well as, That Abraham, our forefather in the flesh, found favor with God? The second question assumes "found" implies that he found "favor" or "righteousness" before God, and that he found such favor with God on the basis of circumcision or even the near-sacrifice of Isaac in Genesis 17 or 22. Paul's question then asks if this is how Abraham ultimately got right with God. Paul's answer is "No!"
2. WordClouds.com. 2023. https://www.wordclouds.com/.

God's Love and Redemptive Peace

1. Songwriters: Christopher C. C. Stafford / Philip Paul Bliss. It Is Well With My Soul lyrics © Bethel Music Publishing, Capitol CMG Publishing, Integrity Music, Universal Music Publishing

Group, Walt Disney Music Company, Warner Chappell Music, Inc.

The Remnant in God's Redemptive Peace

1. The NIV does not put quotation marks around "God did not reject his people" though these words are quoting either 1 Samuel 12:22 or Psalm 94:14. Notice that 1 Samuel 12:22 evokes 8:7 when God informs Samuel that the people have not rejected him but God! Their rejection of God, however, did not lead to God rejecting them. And recall that Paul's other name is "Saul" and that God did give through Samuel a king, and his name was Saul (Wright, "Romans," 675).

The Mystery of God's Redemptive Peace

1. In quoting Isaiah 59:20–21 Paul changes the wording. The OT reads "The Redeemer will come *to* (or *for*) Zion" but Paul shifts it to "The deliverer will come *from* Zion" in Romans 11:26.